CALLIE'S
BISCUITS
and Southern Traditions

CALLIE'S BISCUITS

and Southern Traditions

HEIRLOOM RECIPES FROM OUR FAMILY KITCHEN

Carrie Morey

ATRIA BOOKS

New York   London   Toronto   Sydney   New Delhi

ATRIA BOOKS

A Division of Simon & Schuster, Inc.
1230 Avenue of the Americas
New York, NY 10020

First Atria Books hardcover edition October 2013

ATRIA BOOKS and colophon are trademarks of Simon & Schuster, Inc.

For information about special discounts for bulk purchases,
please contact Simon & Schuster Special Sales at 1-866-506-1949
or business@simonandschuster.com.

The Simon & Schuster Speakers Bureau can bring authors to your
live event. For more information or to book an event contact the
Simon & Schuster Speakers Bureau at 1-866-248-3049 or visit our
website at www.simonspeakers.com.

Designed by Julian Peploe Studio, design assistant: Chie Ushio
Photographs by Angie Mosier, © Carrie Morey, 2013. All rights reserved.
Shutterstock photos on pages 9, 10, 11, 112, 207, and 208

Manufactured in China

10 9 8 7 6 5 4 3 2

Library of Congress Cataloging-in-Publication Data

Morey, Carrie.
  Callie's biscuits and southern traditions : heirloom recipes from our family
kitchen / Carrie Morey.
    pages cm
1. Cooking, American—Southern style. 2. Biscuits. I. Title.
  TX715.2.S68M668 2013
  641.81'57—dc23
                                      2013005964

ISBN 978-1-4767-1321-2
ISBN 978-1-4767-1323-6 (ebook)

This book is dedicated to my families,
both at home and in the bakery—I could not
have done this without your love, support,
and insatiable hunger!

CONTENTS

Chapter 6

...

ENTERTAINING 170

I'd like to say right off the bat that I'm no natural-born biscuit maker. In fact, I never even made biscuits until I was in my thirties. So as you begin to delve into this book and into biscuit making, do not be intimidated by the idea of making amazing biscuits! I know it's a cliché, but in this case it's apt: If I can do it, you can do it.

Growing up, I watched my mother and her mother make biscuits from our family recipe, but I'd never made them myself until I twisted my mother's arm into starting a company with me called Callie's Charleston Biscuits. Baking was not even something I particularly enjoyed at the time, but I figured I could run the business and sales end of Callie's and she could be in charge of the baking. And that's how it went those first couple of years. I would occasionally help out with the biscuit making, but to be honest it was more like going through the motions and doing as I was told rather than putting my heart and soul into it or feeling all that engaged in the process itself.

Then my mom decided to retire.

This had not been a part of my business plan!

Suddenly the landscape of the business shifted, and I was going to have to redouble my efforts. But I was the kind of cook who never measured anything, who loved to improvise and experiment. Biscuits require accuracy, uniformity, and repetition. How in the world could I captain the ship when I didn't know how to sail?

So I dug in, scared as hell, and turned to my employees to teach me how to master every aspect of making the absolute best biscuits. With the business on the line, my previous ambivalence about baking turned into a determined passion. I had to become a baker, and so I did. And I found out I loved it. Almost more than running the business. Making biscuits became second nature to me and now it's as therapeutic as chopping onions and planning menus always have been. Running the business now, I do not get in there with the bakers as much as I'd like—but when I can, I do, and I fit right in. My hands know what to do. And I find myself making biscuits at home with my daughters as well. Before, the thought of making biscuits was daunting, but I now get the urge to make them.

Once you get the technique down, your hands, too, will begin to feel as if they're moving of their own accord. What at first may seem intimidating and infinitely messy will become ritual . . . and maybe a *little* less messy.

Whether I'm performing this ritual with my daughters, my mother, or the Callie's bakers (my other family!), the process always takes on a life of its own after a while. As we plunge our hands into bowls to work the wet dough and roll it out and line the biscuits across the pans, we're telling stories about our day, talking about everything from a recipe conundrum to whom we ran into at the grocery store, and sometimes even airing a grievance or two. When you get to that point with your biscuit making that it becomes almost automatic, you'll be able to concentrate less on each step and more on the conversation and togetherness with your family and friends in the kitchen. And you'll be able to add your own twist to the technique.

Above all, don't worry. If you follow the steps, you really can't mess up biscuits. Biscuits are forgiving. They will get *better* the more you make them and the techniques will get easier. They're not delicate like a pastry. It's okay if they're not perfectly round or they're a little on the big side. So don't put too much pressure on yourself! Enjoy

the process and the taste. The presentation will improve.

I eventually felt ready to experiment with my mother's biscuit recipe, and my first success was my black pepper biscuits. Several of the recipes in the chapter on biscuit making are deliberate variations on the original technique passed down to me. Keep repeating the basic process and you can use the dough and the technique as your canvas to create your own family recipes based on your personal palate and favorite ingredients.

My hope for sharing the gift of biscuit making is to bring a little bit of the old-fashioned baking practices from my grandmothers and mother (those techniques I really never thought I'd master) to your kitchen counter. Even though you're busy, you can enjoy and share these delicious treats. A biscuit is such a tiny little thing, but it has brought a lot to my life, and I hope it can bring goodness to yours as well. There's nothing tastier than a hot one right out of the oven, and that taste is enhanced exponentially by the quality—not necessarily the quantity—of time spent preparing it. For me, there is something indescribably rewarding about creating something so wonderful from such simple ingredients. Something that brings a smile to those I love. It's what makes me want to do it over and over again.

Do I ever get sick of biscuits? No. Would it be an exaggeration to say my life revolves around biscuits? I don't think so. Because for me, biscuits are more than just the end product of the hand mixing, rolling, cutting, and baking. Biscuits are a living legacy of my family history and the women who've gone before me, and with each batch of biscuits I make I'm refining and passing along this legacy to my daughters. Biscuits and family are as inextricably linked in my life as butter and flour. Put them together and something magical happens.

You could even say that "family" is the secret ingredient to *all* my best recipes, not just the biscuits. I like to say, "It's all about the food." That "all the rest" is just extra. But as I thought long and hard about my favorite recipes and techniques and which ones to include in this book, I quickly realized it was people who popped inside my head even before the food. My *mother's* biscuits, my *Mama's* pineapple upside down cake, my *grandmother's* macaroni pie. Even plain boiled shrimp was *Dad's* boiled shrimp. And each recipe brought a story to

Rebecca Maxcey Bailey

mind with it. I really couldn't tell you about Dad's boiled shrimp without telling you about the time his boat and trailer rolled into the creek pulling my grandfather's station wagon with it, or about my mother's perfect tomato sandwiches without telling you about summers spent at the lake with her and her parents, and my grandfather singing Tony Bennett songs to my grandmother.

This passing down of recipes and traditions, this legacy I've inherited, it turns out, is less about the food on the table and more about the people sitting around it—and you wouldn't serve just any food to your favorite people! I serve the food I love, the food I crave to taste and can't wait to make. And as I pass this food with pride down my table of family and friends, I pass along the stories and love of the people who gave it to me.

So who are these people who give me inspiration, stories, and the best food I ever tasted? Well, they are far-flung but extremely tight, diverse in opinion but loyal to one another, and they all treasure gathering around the table for good food and lively conversation. I lived with my father after my parents split up when I was very young, and then both of my parents married wonderful people. My

Caroline Macdowell Hartzog

father and stepmother, Caroline, had a son, Alston, and my mother and stepfather, Tom, had two sons, Kinnon and Miles, so I have three amazing brothers who are a good bit younger than I am. And I have wonderful cousins, aunts, and uncles on all sides. My husband, John, is my perfect match, and we have three girls, Caroline, Cate, and Sarah. I have so many good friends who might as well be family and whose company, stories, and recipes are dear to me as well.

But the matriarchs whose recipes and talents started it all and who laid the foundation for the legacy I hope to build on are my two grandmothers: my father's mother, Mama (pronounced māmă), and my mother's mother, Grandmama (pronounced grandmomma). They couldn't have been more different, and yet they nurtured me, taught me, and fed me with the same degree of love and wisdom.

Mama came from humble roots, but she was a queen in her kitchen. She was one of ten children and with her husband of sixty-six years had six herself: one stillborn baby girl followed by five boys. She never got her driver's license. With five boys and a husband, as my uncle says, it didn't matter whether it was because she loved to cook or there were so many mouths to feed, she was in her kitchen all the time. She was so proud of her boys and loved to watch them play football. Two even earned football scholarships, my father to the University of South Carolina and his youngest brother to The Citadel. There wasn't a lot of money, but she made up for that with love—and plenty of good food. She was a gentle yet incredibly strong woman who was so proud of her children and grandchildren. I miss her.

Grandmama was a fabulous, fabulous cook. She was born and raised in Gaffney, South Carolina, married my grandfather when she was nineteen, and was married for fifty-eight happy years. She was extraordinarily beautiful, bohemian, sophisticated, and intelligent. She taught my mother how to make elegantly small Southern biscuits, and my mother passed her recipes and techniques down to me. Too many of her recipes remain in memory only, as she hardly ever wrote anything down, but I love that trying to re-create them has become a collaborative effort for my girls and me. Maybe in this case the continued conversation about them and the multiple attempts to replicate them makes her legacy even more alive.

My mother, Callie, is the namesake of my business, and her attention to detail and knowing just the right thing to do or fix set a high bar. She is a phenomenal cook, incredibly fashionable, and absolutely gorgeous. She is very liberal and feisty and deep down a true Southern woman despite her worldly ways. I am always asking her for advice on menus, recipes, and entertaining. She's creative and has amazing taste and makes fabulous beautiful food. Even a sandwich tastes better when she makes it!

My father, Donald, is incredibly driven and never takes no for an answer. He grew up in an extremely poor household, and it was only due to his considerable athletic talent that he was able to attend college. He has always taught me to think "I can" and "I will" and has always encouraged and supported me. He's my ultimate hero, and he touches everyone he knows in a positive light.

So as you can see, I come from two very different Southern families. While Grandmama hosted elegant parties, a special occasion at Mama's meant I got to eat at a TV table; I inherited Mama's cast-iron skillet and Grandmama's silver gravy boat. I treasure these women, their wisdom, and their culinary gifts in equal measure, and I hope I make a nice blend of both traditions.

In fact, the dichotomy of my mother's and father's family influences on me is an issue I laugh about almost daily. The other day I was making pickled shrimp for a Carolina tailgate, and sitting there peeling shrimp and deveining each and every one, I was thinking how my dad would no more think of deveining a shrimp than fly to the moon, and my mom would not even consider looking at a shrimp unless it had been deveined—and that about sums it up: my life in a shrimp shell!

My mom would probably say about my cooking and entertaining style that I don't put enough effort into the details. My dad would say I'm too fancy. Luckily, my husband thinks I'm the perfect mix. I try to take the best of all my influences—all my heirlooms—and make them my own to share with my friends, my husband, and my daughters. I think of myself as somewhere in the middle

between fancy and basic, sophistication and salt of the earth: I give my oyster roasts a little flair and my cocktail parties an air of simplicity; I put out boiled peanuts right next to chilled Champagne; and once or twice I may have served Bloody Marys while I was still in my pajamas. I find that there's always a reason to make an ordinary meal a special occasion and always a way to give a special occasion the comfortable, laid-back feel of an ordinary family meal.

I hope that reading this cookbook, you'll be able to take what I share and make it your own, and that some of these recipes will find a place at your family table. And maybe it isn't *all* about the food or making tiny little biscuits, but good food and biscuits isn't such a bad place to start, either.

FAVORITE TOOLS

JUICE GLASS

At Callie's we use two-inch aluminum biscuit cutters, but at home my girls and I use a juice glass. Test some of your juice glasses or shot glasses to see which you like best. Dip the open end in flour to keep it from sticking, and then press out the biscuits from the dough. Not only does this save you from buying and storing yet another kitchen gadget—you're creating a family heirloom. Pretty soon that juice glass will come to be known as the biscuit glass.

ROLLING PIN

At Callie's we use French rolling pins with tapered ends, made from one piece of wood. At our house in Idaho, my rolling pin is the more traditional model with handles. But don't get hung up over this tool. In a pinch I've used a wine bottle. In fact, any cylinder will do. If you are using an improvised rolling pin, put parchment paper between the dough and the cylinder to protect the dough.

DIGITAL THERMOMETER

You only need one thermometer whether you're frying, cooking a roast, or making candy. But it needs to be a good one with a probe attached by a cable. This tool is worth it. It takes away so much guesswork and frustration. It is my best friend when I am frying—I consult it the whole time. With mine, I can set the desired temperature and then leave the temperature probe in whatever is cooking, and when the temperature is reached, it beeps. So much better than standing around holding a thermometer and watching the numbers move. I do not have time for that.

OVEN THERMOMETER

You'd be surprised how inaccurate most oven thermostats are. Especially with biscuits, piecrusts, and cookies, you want to make sure you're not sabotaging yourself with an oven that runs hot or cold. Use an inexpensive oven thermometer to keep tabs on the real oven temperature, and if the thermostat turns out to be pretty far off, call a repairperson to recalibrate it for you.

TONGS

I have maybe five pairs of tongs in different sizes, and I keep them within easy reach in a bin on my counter. I use them for everything from flipping fried chicken to picking up hot bacon to pulling meat out of its bag of marinade without making a mess. Get a nice pair that will last. The springs often break in the cheap ones.

CHARLESTON RICE STEAMER

Mama always had a pot of butter beans and a steamer full of rice on the stove—no matter the time of day or the meal being served. She put soup over rice, okra and tomatoes over rice, and served butter beans over rice with almost everything. Rice in her house was a constant companion to any dish. And even though Mama lived on rural Johns Island in a tiny house with chickens out back, the stovetop rice steamer was just as ubiquitous in the genteel homes of Charleston, with rice on every plate as an accompaniment and in dishes such as hopping john and all kinds of variations of pilau (pronounced pur-low in the South Carolina Lowcountry).

I've had my stovetop rice steamer for ten years, and it delivers fluffy, nonsticky rice every time. The traditional models are aluminum and cost about thirty-five dollars. I have seen some fancier stainless-steel steamers, but the aluminum is just as durable as long as you don't let the water burn out of the bottom. Around Charleston you can find rice steamers in hardware stores and some specialty cooking stores, but you can also find them online. Once you have one, you will enjoy the luxury of mindless rice cooking. No more checking the rice, no more sticky clumps, and no more burning on the bottom. The steamer cooks the rice and then keeps it hot and fluffy until you're ready to use it. Do take note that in a rice steamer you use a ratio of 1 cup of liquid to 1 cup of rice.

VEGETABLE PEELER

A vegetable peeler makes a great cheese slicer for any hard cheese. If I'm grating a bunch of cheese, I use my food processor. If I need just a little, I pull out the peeler and slice or shave it as needed.

TWO KNIVES AND THE BEST SHARPENER IN THE WORLD

Chopped vegetables are a key ingredient for so many of the recipes in this book; even when they aren't the main event or flavor, they create the flavor base for everything from roast chicken to soups. I know a lot of people who avoid cooking just because they find chopping vegetables to be so tiresome, but try it with a really sharp knife and you will be amazed by how much quicker and more fun it is. It can even be meditative at times! In my experience, you only need two knives: a serrated knife for slicing bread and a Santoku-style knife. They don't have to be expensive brands.

The key to chopping is keeping the blade sharp. For this I count on my Chantry brand knife sharpener. I rely on this sharpener so much I pack it in my luggage when I travel and take it with me everywhere I go. I give my knife about twenty passes through the Chantry before I cut anything. I sharpen my knives in the Chantry every day just before I use them. It makes all the difference. You'll look for things to chop just for the fun of it.

WHISK

My whisk is one of the items that I keep on my countertop. It's a necessity for incorporating oil into salad dressings and marinades and for introducing flour into anything liquid. Lump-free gravy just isn't possible without a whisk.

KITCHEN SHEARS

There are times when using scissors is easier than cutting with a knife. I use my shears to cut roasted vegetables, snip fine herbs like dill and thyme, and make smaller bites of almost everything for my children: pizza, chunks of meat, and tortillas, to name a few. Do be sure to use your "food scissors" for food only, and keep them clean.

RESEALABLE PLASTIC BAGS

I go through enough plastic bags to send me to environmental hell. I use them to marinate meats. To store prepped ingredients. To hold homemade pickles in the fridge. To tote snacks. To shake and coat chicken for frying. To keep things in the freezer. I know it's bad. As my penance I do not use any paper towels or paper napkins. And one day I'm going to give up baby wipes, too.

PAPER BAGS

When I don't have my reusable grocery bags, I always ask for paper. I drain bacon and anything fried on paper bags—the bags soak up the grease even better than paper towels. I put fried chicken in a paper bag and stick it back in the oven to keep it warm—and totable. You can shake anything in seasonings or breading in a paper bag. Rediscover these classics if you've forgotten about them; you'll even love their pulpy smell and the loud crunching sound they make as you handle them.

PARCHMENT PAPER

Parchment paper is essential to making my Cinnamon Stickies (page 24). I also like to use it to wrap sandwiches for picnics and other outings. It makes the sandwiches look like they came from a gourmet deli. I love the rustle of the paper as I unwrap one to take a bite! And you can spread the paper out under the sandwich like a placemat to catch the pieces that fall.

IMMERSION BLENDER

Not only is this little gadget hugely helpful for giving soups a smoother texture without having to handle hot liquids in and out of the pot and blender, but it's also handy for smoothies and milkshakes.

VOTIVE CANDLES

I have hundreds of clear glass votive candle holders in my "party closet." They are such an easy and inexpensive way to create a magical atmosphere. Make sure you have one of those long lighters for lighting them, and make sure you plan enough time before the party to light them. Depending on how many you set out, you'd be surprised how long it takes to light them all.

SALT CELLAR AND PEPPER GRINDER

Kosher salt. It's what to use. I use it in all my cooking and baking (I don't even buy any other kind of salt), and I use it to scrub my cast iron when reseasoning is necessary. I keep it in a salt cellar by the stove so it's at my fingertips. My husband likes to say I was raised on a saltlick. I love salt. Keep that in mind when you follow these recipes . . . they may be slightly on the salty side so you may want to adjust accordingly.

Grind your pepper from peppercorns in a pepper grinder. A grinder is not expensive, and it makes all the difference. If you'd rather do all of your grinding at once rather than grinding each time you need it, grind a bunch of pepper and keep it in a bowl or another cellar right next to the salt.

WIRE MESH STRAINER

This tool is sometimes called a "spider skimmer." It has a long bamboo handle and is used a lot in Asian cooking. I use it when frying to remove the food from the hot grease and, more often than not, when I need a colander. For small items this mesh strainer is just right, and there's no need to get out anything bigger that would take up sink space and give you one more thing to clean.

MASON JARS

I use these as glasses, vases, holders for utensils, containers for pickles and olives. I use the smaller wide-mouth four-ounce jars to serve condiments and dips. You can even put votive candles in the short ones. These are on my list of favorite things that I buy very inexpensively at the hardware store.

MINT JULEP CUPS

I use these as the more formal version of mason jars—as glasses, vases, etc. These make a great item to collect. The sterling silver ones are very expensive, but you can find them at antique stores for less. And silver-plated julep cups are very reasonably priced. Both versions shimmer beautifully in candlelight.

LINEN NAPKINS

People give me linen napkins as gifts, and I look for them at flea markets—I love collecting linen cocktail napkins, dinner napkins, and hand towels. I use these at every party I host. They don't need to match—in fact, mixing different colors and embroidery makes the presentation look effortless and authentic.

ROLLS OF WHITE TWINE

Another hardware store staple. I tie it around mason jar vases for a little rustic charm. I wrap linen dinner napkins in twine with a snip of fresh herbs. You can tie a bottle opener to a cooler or tub with it. The possibilities are endless, and one roll will last you many, many parties.

GALVANIZED BUCKETS AND TUBS

You won't believe how much you'll use these indestructible, stackable, washable, charming workhorses. I know I'm repeating myself, but these are yet another hardware store special. Use them to hold ice and cold beer, ice and a bottle of Champagne, boiled peanuts, koozies for beer, kids' drinks, piles of whole fruit and vegetables, and potted plants for an outdoor centerpiece, and to haul things from inside to outside. And you'll find other uses, too. Trust me.

BISCUITS

Grandmama always said, "It's not ladylike to eat a big biscuit." When I heard those words as a child, I can't say I really understood what Grandmama was talking about. Who wouldn't want a big biscuit? And if being ladylike was the price at stake, I was more than willing to forgo that label. But over the years I developed a deep appreciation for the power of a small biscuit and even for the finer points of ladylike behavior—most of the time. And what's crazy is that our family tradition of small biscuits has turned into something bigger than Grandmama or I could ever have imagined. So big, in fact, that I want to share with you the secrets and the stories that pack such a punch into that little treat. These little biscuits have brought big changes to my life, and I hope they might bring you some inspiration as well—or at the very least a happy kitchen and some happy tasters. Because that's what the real secret is all about.

CARRIE'S TIPS

SOUTHERN FLOUR

I use White Lily flour for my biscuits. Even the package is pretty. We stack the bags across almost every wall in Callie's Biscuit House. The elegant, old-fashioned typeface, paired with the bright red seal of the unbleached self-rising variety, gives our walls a cheerful pop of color—not that a biscuit house is ever short on cheer. White Lily is a brand of *Southern flour*, which uses a lower-protein soft winter wheat than your typical flour. If you can't find White Lily for your biscuits, you can use another brand of self-rising flour, but White Lily does make the very best biscuits.

Flour is your friend in biscuit making. More flour does make more mess, but it makes handling the dough so much easier. Don't be afraid to sprinkle more over the dough if it seems too sticky to work with.

HAND MIXING

When we say our biscuits are made by hand, we mean it in every sense of the word. There simply is no better method for mixing biscuit dough than with your bare hands: Mixing with your hands allows for a wet dough that combines ingredients without overmixing. An overworked dough makes for tough biscuits—a hand-mixed, just-combined wet dough makes for the tender, flaky biscuits you're dreaming of when you think about homemade biscuits. Embrace the mess. (If you're not a fan of squishy dough between your fingers, and you decide to sneak a rubber spatula out of the drawer just to test what it would be like to mix the dough with something other than your hands . . . well, I'll never know.)

Born with Butter in My Veins

The other night my girls and I were talking about butter, an occupational hazard and, let's face it, a personal passion. One of my very first food memories is making homemade butter at Memminger Elementary preschool in downtown Charleston. I remember all of us children taking turns at the churn for what seemed like an eternity. I'm not sure if that early experience made me appreciate the goodness of butter or if I was just born this way, but butter is probably my favorite "food." How crazy is it that before the biscuit business was even a blip of an idea, my husband and I got a white English lab and named her Butter? A few years later, my biscuit business was born—a business that uses over 12,000 pounds of butter a year. Butter seems to have been preordained to play a role in my life. And I'm not about to fool with destiny.

Small size I think anyone who's tried a fast-food biscuit would concur with Grandmama's saying: "It's not ladylike to eat a big biscuit." Bite-size biscuits can be plucked from serving trays (or right from the pan) and popped into your mouth with nary a crumb or disintegration in your hands, nor an unbecoming degree of chewing or lip licking. And nobody said you're only allowed to have one.

Testing when in doubt Start checking the color of the biscuits after about 10 minutes or so if you're worried about overbaking or your oven typically bakes hot. You'll also get an idea of when the biscuits are ready by the smell—your nose knows!

CALLIE'S CLASSIC
BUTTERMILK BISCUITS

This is the recipe that started it all. Sitting in my mother's kitchen and watching her prepare the pans of these highly sought-after, melt-in-your-mouth bites of goodness for her catering business gave me the lightning bolt of inspiration for Callie's Charleston Biscuits. It took some convincing to persuade my mother that a biscuit business was a good idea. She was under the impression that people still made their own biscuits! Once I convinced her that the art of biscuit making was far from a daily ritual for most, she warmed to the idea. I don't think she ever dreamed that in a few short years, we'd be making 110,000 biscuits a month and I'd be featured on *The Martha Stewart Show*.

The beauty of this recipe is that biscuit making *can* be part of your family tradition. Just save it for a day when a little bit of a mess in the kitchen won't derail the rest of your plans, because this dough is wet and sticky. If the dough gobs between your fingers with the consistency of pluff mud (what we in the South call marsh mud), don't worry! That's a good sign! Getting my hands dirty is part of the fun for me, but if you are a little more averse to gooey hands, you can certainly use a rubber spatula to mix the dough.

Makes about 10 (2-inch) biscuits

2 cups self-rising flour (White Lily preferred), plus more for dusting
5 tablespoons butter: 4 tablespoons cut in small cubes, at room temperature, and 1 tablespoon melted

¼ cup cream cheese, at room temperature
¾ cup whole buttermilk (may substitute low-fat buttermilk)

1 Preheat the oven to 500°F. Make sure the oven rack is in the middle position.
2 Measure the flour into a large bowl. Incorporate the cubed butter, then the cream cheese into the flour, using your fingers to "cut in" the butter and cheese until the mixture resembles cottage cheese. It will be chunky with some loose flour.
3 Make a well in the center. Pour in the buttermilk and, us-ing your hands or a small rubber spatula, mix the flour into the buttermilk. The dough will be wet and messy.
4 Sprinkle flour on top of the dough. Run a rubber spatula around the inside of the bowl, creating a separation between the dough and the bowl. Sprin-kle a bit more flour in this crease.
5 Flour a work surface or flexible baking mat very well. With force, dump the dough from the bowl onto the surface. Flour the top of the dough and the rolling pin. Roll out the dough to ½-inch thickness into an oval shape. (No kneading is necessary—the less you mess with the dough, the better.)
6 Flour a 2-inch round metal bis-cuit cutter or biscuit glass. Start from the edge of the rolled-out dough and cut straight through the dough with the cutter, trying to maximize the number of bis-

cuits cut from this first roll out. Roll out the excess dough after the biscuits are cut and cut more biscuits. As long as the dough stays wet inside, you can use as much flour on the outside as you need to handle the dough. Place the biscuits on a baking sheet with sides lined with parchment paper, or in a cast-iron skillet, or a baking pan with the biscuit sides touching. (It does not matter what size pan or skillet you use as long as the pan has a lip or sides and the biscuits are touching. If you are using a cast-iron skillet, no parchment paper is necessary.) Brush the tops with the melted butter.

7 Place the pan in the oven and immediately reduce the temperature to 450°F. Bake 16 to 18 minutes, until light brown on top (or as dark as you prefer), rotating the pan once while baking.

Note: You can freeze any leftover biscuits. To reheat, do not defrost. Wrap the biscuits in foil. Bake in a 400°F oven 25 to 30 minutes. Open the top of the foil for the last 3 to 5 minutes to brown a little on top.

BUTTERMILK BLUEBERRY COBBLER

Makes 6 to 8 servings

3 tablespoons butter
2 tablespoons self-rising flour (White Lily preferred)
1 pound fresh or no-sugar-added frozen blueberries
¾ cup white sugar
½ teaspoon pure vanilla extract

¼ teaspoon ground cinnamon
½ teaspoon grated lemon zest
2 teaspoons fresh lemon juice
10 frozen buttermilk biscuits, not thawed (use your favorite brand—that's Callie's Charleston Biscuits, right?)

1 tablespoon turbinado sugar
Serving suggestion (optional): Whipped Cream (page 26) or vanilla ice cream

1 Preheat the oven to 350°F.
2 Melt the butter in an 8½- to 9-inch cast-iron skillet or pie dish. Reserve 1 tablespoon of the melted butter.
3 Add the flour to the butter in the pan and mix until a smooth paste forms. Add blueberries, white sugar, vanilla, and cinnamon and mix well. Stir in the lemon zest and juice. Top with the biscuits. Brush the biscuit tops with the reserved melted butter and sprinkle with the turbinado sugar.
4 Cover with aluminum foil. Bake 25 minutes.

5 Remove the foil and bake 5 minutes more to allow the biscuit tops to turn light brown in color.
6 Serve warm, topped with whipped cream or ice cream, if you wish.

BLACK PEPPER
BISCUITS

Once I mastered my mother's buttermilk biscuit recipe, I was ready to experiment a little and put my own savory edge on things. You can experiment, too! Start small like I did with the black pepper. Try adding one element, and go from there. Try minced fresh herbs, cooked crumbled sausage, minced country ham. Even if it's not perfect the first time, it will certainly be tasty. And keep trying and adjusting until you get it just the way you want it.

These black pepper biscuits have the same luscious texture as the original, but with a little kick to them that really excites the palate. Even though they are savory, don't let that keep you from serving them for breakfast or with jam. That savory/sweet contrast is delightful. For cocktail parties I like to serve them as small sandwiches with a little bit of meat inside.

Makes about 10 (2-inch) biscuits

2 cups self-rising flour (White Lily preferred), plus more for dusting
1½ to 2 tablespoons coarsely ground black pepper
5 tablespoons butter: 4 tablespoons cut in small cubes, at room temperature, and 1 tablespoon melted
¼ cup cream cheese, at room temperature
¾ cup whole buttermilk (may substitute low-fat buttermilk)
Topping: 1½ teaspoons kosher salt and 1½ teaspoons coarsely ground black pepper, mixed

1 Preheat the oven to 500°F. Make sure the oven rack is in the middle position.

2 Measure the flour into a large bowl. Mix in the pepper to distribute evenly. Incorporate the cubed butter and then the cream cheese into the flour, using your fingers to "cut in" the butter and cheese until the mixture resembles cottage cheese. It will be chunky with some loose flour.

3 Make a well in the center. Pour in the buttermilk and, using your hands, mix the flour into the buttermilk. The dough will be wet and messy.

4 Sprinkle flour on top of the dough. Run a rubber spatula around the inside of the bowl, creating a separation between the dough and the bowl. Sprinkle a bit more flour in this crease.

5 Flour a work surface or flexible baking mat very well. With force, dump the dough from the bowl onto the surface. Flour the top of the dough and the rolling pin. Roll out the dough to ½-inch thickness into an oval shape. (No kneading is necessary—the less you mess with the dough, the better.)

6 Flour a 2-inch round metal biscuit cutter or biscuit glass. Start from the edge of the rolled-out dough and cut straight through the dough with the cutter, trying to maximize the number of biscuits cut from this first roll out. Roll out the excess dough after the biscuits are cut and cut more biscuits. As long as the dough stays wet inside, you can use as much flour on the outside as you need to handle the dough. Place the biscuits on a baking sheet with sides lined with parchment paper, in a cast-iron skillet, or a baking pan with the biscuit sides touching. (It does not matter what size pan or skillet you use as long as the pan has a lip or sides and the biscuits are touching. If you are using a cast-iron skillet, no parchment paper is necessary.) Brush the tops with the melted butter and sprinkle with the topping.

7 Place the pan in the oven and immediately reduce the temperature to 450°F. Bake 16 to 18 minutes, until light brown on top (or as dark as you prefer), rotating the pan once while baking.

MAMA'S CAST-IRON
YEAST BISCUITS

While my mother's biscuits were elegant special-occasion delights destined for wedding receptions and cocktail parties, my grandmother Mama's biscuits were an everyday pleasure, always on hand to accompany any meal, any conversation, or any call for celebration, comfort, or bucking-up. Staying over at her house as a child, if I ate all my supper I got to punch a hole in one of her yeast biscuits with my thumb and fill it with pancake syrup as a special treat. That motivation worked every time.

This dough lasts in the refrigerator for a few days, so you can follow Mama's lead and keep the dough on hand to pull out and bake as needed. Hot biscuits on demand—a tradition well worth keeping. Do yourself a favor and never eat a biscuit again unless it's hot! This recipe is an easy way to do just that.

Makes about 36 biscuits

---

2 (¼-ounce) packages active dry yeast
½ cup sugar
¼ cup warm water

5 cups all-purpose flour (White Lily preferred), plus more for dusting
1 tablespoon baking powder (aluminum-free preferred)

1 teaspoon baking soda
1 teaspoon kosher salt
1 cup vegetable shortening
1 to 1½ cups buttermilk

---

1 Preheat the oven to 400°F. Make sure the oven rack is in the middle position. You do not need to grease the cast-iron skillet. You will need to bake in batches or save remaining cut biscuits to bake at a later time.
2 Combine the yeast, 1 teaspoon of the sugar, and the water in a 2-cup liquid measuring cup, stirring to dissolve the yeast.
3 Whisk together the flour, the remaining sugar, the baking powder, baking soda, and salt in a large bowl. Use your fingers to "cut in" the shortening into the flour until the mixture resembles Parmesan cheese.
4 Make a well in the center and

pour in the yeast mixture and 1 cup of the buttermilk. Using your hands, mix the flour into the liquids. The dough should be wet. Work in more buttermilk if the dough is dry.
5 Sprinkle flour on top of the dough. Run a rubber spatula around the inside of the bowl, creating a separation between the dough and the bowl. Sprinkle a bit more flour in this crease.
6 Flour a work surface or flexible baking mat very well. With force, dump the dough from the bowl onto the surface. Flour your hands and press out the dough into a rectangle

until the dough gets to ½-inch thickness.
7 Flour a 2½-inch round metal biscuit cutter. Start from the edge of the rolled-out dough and cut straight through the dough with the cutter. Place the biscuits in a 9-inch cast-iron skillet with their sides touching. (Any size skillet is fine as long as the sides of the biscuits are touching.) Let rest 15 minutes while the dough rises.
8 Bake 12 to 15 minutes, until golden brown.

Note: Unbaked cut biscuits will keep in the fridge for 4 to 5 days. Take out as needed and bake as directed above.

MOM'S CINNAMON STICKIES (MY VERSION)

Sunday brunch at my mother's has always been a cherished if wonderfully harried tradition. These days there are usually nine or so people ranging in age from four to sixty-three, all of us in the kitchen, helping. My stepfather, Tom, has usually just come in from some kind of exercise adventure and is pulling out the Fritos, Cheez-Its, and peanut butter, frantically snacking as my mother stirs the grits. My brother Kinnon is making his perfectly crisp pancakes, and my girls are grating cheese for the grits. All of us have huge personalities, and we're all talking over one another until we

STICKIES

2 cups self-rising flour (White Lily preferred), plus more for dusting
⅓ cup white sugar
⅓ cup packed light brown sugar
14 tablespoons (1¾ sticks) butter: 8 tablespoons cut in cubes, at room temperature, and 6 tablespoons melted
¼ cup cream cheese, at room temperature
¾ cup whole buttermilk, plus 1 tablespoon if needed (may substitute low-fat buttermilk)

TOPPING

1 cup chopped pecans
⅓ cup white sugar
⅓ cup packed light brown sugar
1 tablespoon ground cinnamon

1 Line a baking sheet with parchment paper and flour the paper generously.
2 Measure the flour into a large bowl. Mix in the white and brown sugars. Incorporate the cubed butter and then the cream cheese into the flour, using your fingers to "cut in" the butter and cheese until the mixture resembles chunky cottage cheese.
3 Make a well in the center. Pour in the buttermilk and, using your hands or a small rubber spatula, mix the flour into the buttermilk. The dough will be wet and messy.
4 Sprinkle flour on the dough and turn the dough onto the parchment paper. Press into a rectangle. Flour the top gener-ously and roll out to a ¼-inch thickness into a rectangle. Use a pastry brush to brush excess flour from the dough.
5 Brush the surface with 4 table-spoons of the melted butter.
6 Make the topping: Stir together all the ingredients. Sprinkle two-thirds of the topping over the dough.
7 With well-floured hands, work-ing from a long side, begin rolling the dough into a log, using the parchment paper to lift and roll the dough. Smooth the dough, and keeping it on the baking sheet, freeze for 45 minutes.
8 While the log is freezing, preheat the oven to 500°F. Put parchment paper on a baking sheet. If using a cast-iron skillet, no greasing or parchment paper is necessary.
9 Trim the ends of the log and cut in ½-inch-thick slices, using a serrated knife. (Flouring the knife will help cut through the dough.)
10 Lay the stickies flat on the prepared pan. Brush with the remaining 2 tablespoons melted butter and sprinkle with the remaining topping.
11 Place in the oven and imme-diately reduce the oven tem-perature to 400°F. Bake 16 to 18 minutes, rotating the pan once, until golden brown.
12 Serve warm.

Note: You can make, shape, and top these the night before and keep in the fridge to bake in the morning.

finally come together and sit down to the beautiful table spread with grits, pancakes, tomato pie, and stickies. We're all silent for a moment as we take those first few bites of comfort, home, supreme deliciousness . . . and then it starts up again! Everyone talking over everyone else and explaining the escapades and misadventures of the night before.

I love every chaotic minute of it. These stickies are one of my mother's many specialties and an essential element of our Sunday brunches. She never writes anything down, so this is my best interpre-tation of her recipe. Forget any notions of over-sized shopping mall cinnamon rolls—these bites are sweet but not too sweet, with the texture of a biscuit. And on the rare occasion when I may have been overserved a cocktail or two, these stickies are what I crave when I wake up the next morning. They taste good any time of day for any occasion, but a little bit of Sunday morning family "conversa-tion" does seem to bring out their sweetness even more.

Makes 10 to 12 stickies

SOUTHERN SHORTCAKES

I'm not sure how those packaged yellow cake cups became associated with shortcake, but rest assured that even for a busy person, those are not the only shortcake option! This wonderful recipe really took shape when the Callie's bakers had some ideas for improving my mother's already tasty shortcake recipe that we had been using, by creating a crustier top to offset the slightly dense texture. With the addition of turbinado sugar, these cakes have a crunch and sugary sparkle that will stand up to even the juiciest summer berries. Turbinado sugar is what's also known as "raw sugar." It's darker in color than refined sugar and the grains are a little larger. Sugar in the Raw is a familiar brand, but other brands are available as well.

Makes about 12 (3-inch) shortcakes

- 2 cups self-rising flour (White Lily preferred), plus more for dusting
- ⅓ cup white sugar
- 7 tablespoons butter: 6 tablespoons cut in small cubes, at room temperature, and 1 tablespoon melted
- ½ to ¾ cup whole milk
- 1 teaspoon pure vanilla extract
- 1 tablespoon turbinado sugar

MACERATED FRUIT

Macerate is just a fancy word for a very simple process.

1 Slice berries or other fruit into a bowl.
2 Sprinkle just a little vanilla extract and a little sugar over the fruit.
3 Mix the berries with the sugar and vanilla.
4 Cover the bowl and let the fruit sit in the refrigerator for up to 2 hours.

WHIPPED CREAM

- 1 pint heavy whipping cream
- ¼ teaspoon pure vanilla extract
- 2 teaspoons sugar

1 Chill the mixer beaters and bowl in the freezer for 20 minutes or longer.
2 Whip the cream for 2 to 3 minutes, starting at low speed and increasing to high speed, until it's fluffy and light. Add the vanilla and sugar and whip until soft peaks form.
3 Store in the refrigerator until it's time to serve, up to 3 days.

Note: You can also whip the cream by hand with a whisk. This is a great way to exhaust little helpers in the kitchen!

1 Preheat the oven to 450°F.

2 Measure the flour into a large bowl. Mix in the white sugar. Incorporate the cubed butter into the flour, using your fingers to "cut in" the butter until the mixture resembles cottage cheese. It will be chunky with some loose flour.

3 Stir together the milk and vanilla. Make a well in the center of the dough. Pour in the milk and, using your hands or a small rubber spatula, mix the flour into the milk. The dough will be wet and messy.

4 Sprinkle flour on top of the dough. Run a rubber spatula around the inside of the bowl, creating a separation between the dough and the bowl. Sprinkle a bit more flour in this crease.

5 Flour a work surface or flexible baking mat very well. With force, dump the dough from the bowl onto the surface. Flour the top of the dough and the rolling pin. Roll out the dough to ½-inch thickness into an oval shape. (No kneading is necessary—the less you mess with the dough, the better.)

6 Flour a 3-inch round metal biscuit cutter or biscuit glass. Start from the edge of the rolled-out dough and cut straight through the dough with the cutter, trying to maximize the number of biscuits cut from this first roll out. Roll out the excess dough after the biscuits are cut and cut more biscuits. As long as the dough stays wet inside, you can use as much flour on the outside as you need to handle the dough. Place the biscuits on an ungreased baking sheet with the biscuit sides touching. Brush the tops with the melted butter. Sprinkle with the turbinado sugar.

7 Bake 16 to 18 minutes, rotating the pan once while baking, until golden brown. To serve, cut the shortcakes in half, put macerated fruit and whipped cream on the bottom halves, put the tops on the shortcakes (sandwich-style), and then drizzle juice from the macerated fruit on the tops.

SHORTCAKE TRIFLE

Makes 8 servings

6 shortcakes (Callie's Charleston Biscuits Shortcakes, or Southern Shortcakes, page 26), thawed if frozen

2 tablespoons butter, melted
1 teaspoon turbinado sugar
4 cups fresh berries (mixed or all one kind, raspberries and blackberries preferred), rinsed and drained

2 teaspoons white sugar, or more if the berries are not sweet
Whipped Cream (page 26)

1 Preheat the oven to 375°F.

2 Crumble the shortcakes onto a baking sheet and sprinkle with the butter and turbinado sugar. Bake about 15 minutes, or until crunchy and golden brown. Let cool on the sheet on a cooling rack.

3 If using strawberries, cut in quarters. Sprinkle the berries with the white sugar and refrigerate for up to 2 hours.

4 Layer your trifle in a glass bowl. Start with a layer of whipped cream, then berries, then shortcake. Repeat, using up the ingredients. Finish with a layer of whipped cream and the small crumbs that remain from the crumbled shortcakes. Serve immediately.

CALLIE'S BAKERS

When I hear other business owners talk about dealing with employees, they don't always make it sound like a positive experience. I cannot say enough how thankful I am for my team of bakers at Callie's. They were the ones who coached me into biscuit-making mastery with their expertise and their gentle guidance on the finer points of the process. "That's a little too fat" or "that's a little too thin," they'd tell me as I'd roll out the dough another time hoping this would be the batch where I'd know I'd finally perfected it.

There is a constant chatter among the six of us as we work. Not only are we talking about what's going on in our lives, but we are also always brainstorming. I've mentioned several times that the key to making biscuits is following the method and practic-

ing it over and over again. And the bakers and I stay true to this concept, but there is an immense amount of creativity and inventiveness buzzing as we constantly try to get better and create new tastes and products we love and think our customers will love.

So I guess you could say the Callie's bakers really aren't like employees at all. They are more like a sisterhood. Because of them, I can travel and never worry that production will slow or the quality will go down. They are as demanding about perfection as I am! How many business owners can say that about their employees? They each have vision, enthusiasm, knowledge, and wisdom, and together they make a dynamo team. I think you can taste their talent and love for what they do in every biscuit that goes out Callie's door. I savor that taste every day.

BISCUIT BAR

When *Garden & Gun* magazine hosted a party for its exclusive Secret Society club to celebrate the opening of the prestigious Keeneland Horse Races in Lexington, Kentucky, they selected Callie's Charleston Biscuits as a headline feature of the menu, chosen for its status as a "Southern icon." Being deemed an icon by the arbiter of good taste in the South is hardly an everyday occurrence, so I was extremely proud and appreciative. And I was also inspired by the *way* they served my little icons: as part of a biscuit bar with all sorts of scrumptious toppings.

A biscuit bar is a great idea for a party— guests love to pick and choose their own toppings. I use this same guest participation tactic for soup parties and Bloody Mary bars as well (see pages 96 and 212). Set up a biscuit bar for a brunch or any daytime get-together. Or think of the topping ideas as even more ways to enjoy your biscuits any day.

You probably already have the ingredients for most of these toppings. And the whipped butters are also versatile. Try the savory variation on bagels, steaks, and baked potatoes and the sweet on everything from toast to waffles to sweet potatoes. You can shape the butter into a log, wrap it in plastic, and freeze to keep on hand. When you include meat on your biscuit bar, be sure to cut it into small enough bits to fit the biscuit properly.

Basket of warm biscuits, all plain buttermilk or a variety
Toppings: *Thinly sliced country ham, fried chicken, pork loin, beef tenderloin, pimento cheese, sorghum syrup, honey, high-quality jams and preserves, Ham Salad (page 112), BBQ Chicken Salad (see page 110), Savory Whipped Butter (recipe follows), Cinnamon Butter (page 31), and Smoked Sausage with Spicy Mustard Mayo (page 30)*

SAVORY WHIPPED BUTTER

Makes about ⅔ cup

8 tablespoons (1 stick) butter, at room temperature
1 clove garlic, minced
2 tablespoons minced green onion (1 onion, white and green parts)

1 teaspoon minced fresh thyme, or more to taste
Kosher salt and freshly ground black pepper (more than you think you'll need)

1 Combine all the ingredients in a bowl with a rubber spatula, or whip with a handheld mixer.

2 Transfer to a ramekin, cover with plastic wrap, and store in the fridge, or roll into a log on plastic wrap and freeze until ready to use.

SMOKED SAUSAGE
WITH SPICY MUSTARD MAYO

Makes 1⅔ cups mayo and enough sausage for 24 biscuits

SPICY MUSTARD MAYO
1 cup mayonnaise
⅓ cup sour cream
¼ cup Dijon mustard
¼ cup chopped green onions (about 2 onions, white and green parts)

2 tablespoons chopped fresh flat-leaf parsley
4 to 6 dashes hot sauce
Freshly ground black pepper

SAUSAGE
1 (13-ounce) link high-quality kielbasa or other smoked sausage
½ teaspoon vegetable oil

1 Make the spicy mustard mayo: Combine the mayonnaise, sour cream, mustard, green onions, and parsley.
2 Let the flavors marry for about 30 minutes.
3 Add the hot sauce and black pepper.

4 Prepare the sausage: Slice the sausage into 24 rounds.
5 Heat the vegetable oil in a cast-iron skillet. Cook the sausage rounds until well browned, 3 to 4 minutes per side. Cook in two batches to avoid overcrowding.
6 Drain the rounds on a paper bag. To serve, slice the biscuits,

spread the spicy mustard mayo on the inside of the tops and bottoms, put the sausage rounds on the bottoms, and add the tops (sandwich-style).

Note: I prefer my sausage crisp and almost burnt for more flavor.

CINNAMON BUTTER

Makes about ⅔ cup

8 tablespoons (1 stick) butter, at room temperature
1 teaspoon ground cinnamon

1 tablespoon light brown sugar
1½ tablespoons white sugar

1 Combine all the ingredients in a bowl with a rubber spatula, or whip with a handheld mixer.

2 Transfer to a ramekin, cover with plastic wrap, and store in the fridge, or roll into a log on plastic wrap and freeze until ready to use.

NATHALIE DUPREE'S
BISCUIT PANZANELLA SALAD

This perfect savory recipe for enjoying leftover biscuits is courtesy of my friend and mentor Nathalie Dupree and appears in her fantastic book *Southern Biscuits*. Nathalie is a true chef—her *Mastering the Art of Southern Cooking* is the new bible of Southern cooking, and her expertise, knowledge, and passion for the culinary arts are only surpassed by her kindness and willingness to help those of us hoping to glean a little bit of her wisdom and abilities. She is always reminding me how important it is for women in the food industry to support each other, and she leads this effort by example. No matter what I ask her, whether it's about a certain technique or for general advice, she always opens her door to me and gives me her time, encouragement, and guidance. Nathalie's so good to let me "borrow" this recipe—I love it so much, if it were something less shareable, I don't think I'd be able to convince myself to give it back.

Makes 6 to 8 servings

4½ cups torn or cut biscuits, in 2-inch pieces
1½ tablespoons olive oil
4 medium tomatoes, coarsely chopped

1 small onion, thinly sliced
2 tablespoons chopped fresh basil

2 tablespoons chopped fresh lemon balm (may substitute 1 tablespoon lemon zest)
2 to 3 tablespoons fresh lemon juice

1 Preheat the oven to 400°F.
2 Place the biscuit pieces in a large bowl and sprinkle with 1½ teaspoons of the olive oil. Toss lightly.
3 Spread out the biscuit pieces on a baking sheet and toast in the oven for 15 minutes, or until tinged with brown.
4 Remove the biscuits to a large serving bowl. Add the remaining 1 tablespoon olive oil, the tomatoes, onion, basil, lemon balm, and lemon juice, and toss to combine.

Note: This salad is best enjoyed the day it's made.

BUTTERMILK BISCUIT CROUTONS

Makes 3 to 4 cups

8 prepared, leftover, or purchased buttermilk biscuits

8 tablespoons (1 stick) butter, at room temperature

3 teaspoons smoked paprika
⅛ teaspoon kosher salt

1 Preheat the oven to 400°F.
2 Separate the biscuits into uneven chunks. Place in a cast-iron skillet or metal pie dish. Combine the butter, paprika, and salt and mix well. Spread over the top of the biscuits. Crisp in the hot oven for about 12 minutes, until golden brown, or more if you prefer a crisper crouton.

3 Serve on salads and soups. Store leftovers in an airtight container for up to 3 days.

CALLIE'S BISCUIT HOUSE

Our Callie's Charleston Biscuits home for the first five years of the business was a tiny house we'd converted into a commercial kitchen. We loved the house, but the lease was coming due. Not only that, we were busting at the seams, as we were lucky enough to be getting more and more orders for biscuits, as well as creating new products. So I reluctantly went on the search for a new bakery. There were plenty of properties for lease at the time, and I found several that matched what I could afford with the amount of space I needed. But it was going to be a real adjustment to go from our cozy little house to a factory-type space with tiny if any windows, concrete floors, and metal walls. I was just about to sign a lease on a warehouse in a strip of warehouses when I realized I couldn't commit until I tried one more thing.

A friend of mine worked in a space on the old Charleston Navy Base that had been converted to private property. As far as I knew, there were only warehouses out there, too, but at least they were *old* warehouses and maybe they would have some kind of personality or some neat old brick or something I could cling to as more charming than a vinyl box.

The only available property on the base within my price range wasn't a warehouse at all, but rather an old house that had been living quarters for navy officers and their families. And it wasn't for lease. It was for sale. We drove up, and before I even got out of the car I knew it was perfect. But I didn't know if I was ready to buy something. That felt like a huge jump. My father and step-mother, however, encouraged me to make the commitment and create a place for Callie's Charleston Biscuits to call home. My father has always been such a mentor to me. I had dreams and goals, but he had a real vision; he was able to see what the business could become, and he gave me the confidence to move forward. I couldn't have done it without them.

The house is ninety-five years old. It has a wraparound porch. Huge windows. A fireplace. Original hardwood floors—the color of golden brown, just-out-of-the-oven biscuits, no less. There are plaques listing the names of all the navy families who have lived there. It is anything but industrial. I knew it would be the perfect place to bring biscuits into the world.

Biscuit making is a part of Southern history and making biscuits inside a building with its own history just feels right. The house had "cook's quarters," so we know the house included live-in help for the officers' families. I am convinced those cooks were making biscuits for the families they served, and that continuity of artisans gives the house an authentic sense, even a feeling of know-how and authority that we are where we are supposed to be and doing what we were meant to do. When I drive up to Callie's Biscuit House, I can't help but smile. In fact, it gives me a feeling very similar to the one I get when I bite into a hot buttery biscuit.

SKILLET AND STOVETOP

Whenever my grandmother Mama pulled on one of her floral house-coats that hung on the back of her bedroom door, I knew she was headed to the kitchen to make something wonderful, usually in her cast-iron skillet. She fed her five sons and all of their children from that skillet—spirit-lifting food like yeast biscuits, pineapple upside-down cake, fried chicken, and fried bologna for sandwiches on white bread with mayo. When I inherited the skillet, I treasured it for everything it brought to mind: Mama standing at her avocado-green stove, the percolator on the counter always full of coffee, the comfort and warmth of her cozy kitchen in her tiny house, and the loving touch she bestowed upon everything she fed her family. But I had no idea where that skillet would lead, the dishes I would come to create with it, or that I would one day be writing a cookbook chapter based on the techniques Mama had taught me and the food she fed me. You'd think her skillet had some kind of magic, but what it really possesses is the taste of a family history's worth of good cooking. And maybe that *is* some kind of magic, the magic of seasoning.

Seasoning is the process by which the cast iron develops layers of grease that over time form a coating, giving the cast iron its black color and nonstick surface. The seasoning continues every time it's used, with every dish made inside it adding another coat of smoothness that improves the skillet's performance and deepens the flavor of its contents. Everything Mama fixed in her skillet seeped its way into the cast iron itself, seasoning every meal I now make in it. And every one of those meals I make in the skillet for my own family gives it one more layer of flavor, one more recipe to keep, one more story to tell. To me it's a family heirloom that I hold as dear as any jewels and that I expect my girls to fight over after I'm gone.

Lest you worry that your pots and pans lack the bacon-greased legacy of Mama's, you can start seasoning your own family jewel without a whole lot of effort or money. Really. Go into any hardware store and for twenty-five dollars you can get a made-in-the-USA cast-iron skillet. You can get a small one for twelve. I am not kidding. It's that easy to go from boring cookware to establishing a new technique for cooking and a family tradition you'll want to pass down to your children.

Even though I cherish Mama's skillet, it's not a relic hanging on my wall—it sits on top of my stove permanently. I use it that much. You can use yours that much, too. In fact, the more you use it, the better it gets. Even though I make my living making food, you'd be amazed by how few pots, pans, and kitchen gadgets I use or even have. If I can't use it for more than one thing, then I really don't need it. My cast iron is second only to my hands in the number of ways I use it in my kitchen. Besides the sentimental value, besides the economic value, the key to its versatility is the fact that *it can go right from the stove to the oven* since it's all one piece of nearly indestructible cast iron. This means a crispier crust on everything. It means never under- or overcooking fried chicken. It rights—or should I say *prevents*—cooking wrongs by heating its contents evenly, maintaining a steady temperature, and allowing you to finish any dish in the oven.

When I discovered how versatile and easy to use Mama's skillet was, I couldn't wait to start experimenting. Unfortunately the skillet was not big enough to hold the chicken I wanted to roast. So off to the hardware store I went to get a bigger one, and I started looking around. I couldn't believe what I saw: old-fashioned aluminum rice steamers, ice cream churns, nut crackers, can openers—I had no idea. Now I go to the hardware store for my glassware, too. I use mason jars as wineglasses, juice glasses, jars to store and shake salad dressings, vases for cut flowers, and, of course, for pickling as well. What's old became new for me that day in the hardware store, and I've since become keen on the ways that traditional products, ingredients, and techniques can be adapted to fit modern life and add value and texture to it.

I wonder what Mama would think of some of the Asian dishes I make in her skillet or the fact that I use cinnamon in my fried chicken seasoning.

Even though cast iron is such a Southern icon, its applications are universal. Asian, Mexican, Indian, Mediterranean—it's all good in the skillet. So take the techniques I discuss in this chapter and go with it. Experiment with your own favorite or local ingredients. Try lobster instead of shrimp, asparagus instead of green beans.

If you ever mess up and think you've ruined your cast iron, don't worry. You get to reseason it and start all over again (more about this process in the tips section of this chapter). These skillets are regenerative not only in themselves but to the food, to the palate, and to the family. There's something a little spiritual about cooking for the ones you love (most days, anyway)—in this case a spirit that's been passed down via a heavy black skillet. I'm not saying that cooking in cast iron is going to transform your dinner table into an island of peace and happiness, but I am saying that cooking in cast iron may open up your culinary possibilities like it did for me. And you never know where those possibilities might take you.

This chapter is full of the versatile, maybe even unexpected, ways to use cast iron beyond the obligatory skillet cornbread. But let me tell you, there's a reason that skillet cornbread already has such a widespread reputation. Try my grandmother Mama's recipe and you'll taste why yourself. Mama also had a cast-iron cornstick pan that baked the batter into sticks of cornbread shaped like ears of corn. She'd make the cornsticks every time she made her vegetable soup. The cast iron gave the sticks such a crust they tasted almost fried. I would dip them into the vegetable soup and savor each bite as it melted in my mouth. Unfortunately I did not inherit Mama's cornstick pan, but if you have one, you can use this recipe to make the cornsticks. The next best thing to those cornsticks, though, is the skillet corncakes variation . . . soooo good with vegetable soup. They don't taste fried—they *are* fried.

CAST-IRON BUTTERMILK CORNBREAD

Makes 8 to 10 servings

3 slices bacon
1¼ cups plus 2 teaspoons cake flour or all-purpose flour
¾ cup fine-grind yellow cornmeal
¼ cup sugar
2 teaspoons baking powder

1 teaspoon kosher salt
½ teaspoon freshly ground black pepper
1 cup whole or low-fat buttermilk
⅓ cup whipping cream
1 large egg, beaten

OPTIONAL
4 green onions, chopped (white and green parts)
1½ cups shredded sharp cheddar cheese

1 Preheat the oven to 400°F.
2 Cook the bacon in a cast-iron skillet. Drain the bacon on a paper bag, keeping the bacon drippins in the skillet. Crumble the bacon to add to the batter, or use for another purpose.
3 Whisk together the flour, cornmeal, sugar, baking powder, salt, and pepper in a large bowl. In a separate bowl, combine the buttermilk, cream, and egg and add to the dry ingredients. Mix well.
4 Return the skillet with the drippins to high heat until very hot but not smoking. Pour in the batter and sprinkle with the bacon, green onions, and/or cheese, if you wish.
5 Bake 20 minutes, or until a toothpick inserted in the center comes out clean. Store leftovers in an airtight container.

SKILLET CORNCAKES
Makes 8 to 12 corncakes

1 Prepare the basic batter as on page 38, step 3.
2 Heat the skillet until hot. Pour in 2 teaspoons vegetable oil and spread with a brush to coat the pan. Carefully pour out any excess oil.
3 Pour ¼ cup batter into the pan for each corn-cake. Cook 2 to 3 minutes per side, until you see small bubbles in the center of a cake and the edges get toasty brown.
4 Flip and cook the other side. Put the corn-cakes in a 200°F oven to keep warm.
5 Repeat until all the batter is used, adding oil to the pan as needed.

VEGETABLE-BEEF SOUP

Makes 8 to 10 servings

⅓ cup all-purpose flour
1½ teaspoons kosher salt, plus more for seasoning
1½ teaspoons freshly ground black pepper, plus more for seasoning
2 pounds beef stew meat or chuck, cut in ½-inch cubes
Vegetable oil, to sear meat

1 tablespoon butter
1 tablespoon olive oil
1½ cups chopped carrots (about 6 carrots)
1½ cups chopped celery (about 4 stalks)
1½ cups chopped onion (1 large onion)
2 cloves garlic, smashed

1 (28-ounce) can diced tomatoes
Up to 2 cups water
2 quarts beef stock
4 cups vegetables of your choice: sliced okra, corn kernels, cut green beans, shelled lima beans, butter beans, and/or peas

1 Prepare the seasoned flour: Mix the flour, salt, and pepper in a large resealable plastic bag.
2 Working in batches if necessary, add the meat, seal the bag, and shake the bag to coat the cubes well.
3 Heat a thin layer of vegetable oil in a large skillet on medium-high heat. Cook the meat in batches, if necessary, turning a few times, until seared and brown. Do not crowd the pan. Remove the meat with a wire

mesh strainer and set aside. Pour out any excess fat, but do not wash the skillet.
4 In a stockpot or large saucepan, melt the butter into the olive oil. Add the carrots, celery, and onion and cook, stirring from time to time, until the onion is soft, about 8 minutes.
5 Stir in the garlic and the tomatoes and their juices, using the water to rinse all the tomatoes into the soup. Add the meat.

6 Pour some of the stock into the skillet and bring to a boil on medium heat. Scrape up the browned bits and add to the soup.
7 Add the rest of the stock to the soup. Add the vegetables of your choice. Bring to a boil, reduce the heat, and simmer 1½ to 2½ hours. Taste the meat for tenderness after 1½ hours.
8 Taste and adjust the salt and pepper.

CARRIE'S TIPS

SEASONING AND CARE OF CAST-IRON SKILLETS

Do not be afraid of a cast-iron skillet unless someone is threatening to hit you over the head with it. The directions always say *don't do this, don't do that,* but the reality is that you cannot screw it up other than by putting it in the dishwasher. Even if your cast iron rusts or you find yourself having to scrub it for some reason, you can always bring it back to life.

These days, most cast-iron skillets, including the Lodge brand, are sold already seasoned, but some come unseasoned. The unseasoned ones are steel-gray rather than black. To season a brand-new skillet or other cast-iron implement for the first time, first wash it out with soap and water and dry it with a cloth. Put it in a 200°F oven for a minute or two just to be sure all of the water has evaporated from its surface. Raise the oven temperature to 350°F. Rub olive oil (or any kind of oil) over the entire piece—inside and out and the handle as well. Put a baking sheet or aluminum foil on the bottom rack of the oven to catch any drips, then put the coated piece upside down on a rack above. Let it stay in the oven for an hour. Turn off the oven but let the skillet stay in the oven for a while to dry out and cool. It may smell smoky.

• Avoid washing and scrubbing seasoned cast iron with soap and never let it near the dishwasher. But cleaning it is even easier than using the dishwasher. Simply wipe out the cast iron and dry it.

• I may be alone on this, but I do not like cooking eggs in the skillet. Every now and then I find my husband in the kitchen frying an egg in one, which annoys me to no end. For some reason the eggy film sticks, and I end up having to use soap and water rather than a baby wipe. Not a happy cook when that happens.

• If you do get something stuck on your cast iron that won't come off, first try putting ¼ inch of water in the pan, bring it to a boil, and gently scrape up the bits as the water boils, as if deglazing the pan. If that doesn't work, use kosher salt as an abrasive to rub it off. And if *that* doesn't work, use a scrub brush and a little soap. Do what it takes and then you can reseason it.

• To reseason cast iron after having to use soap or because of rust, first remove any rust with steel wool or a brush, rinse it with water, and dry it with a cloth. Make sure the cast iron is completely dry by putting it in a 200°F oven for a minute or two. Coat the cast iron with olive oil and rub the inside with kosher salt and some freshly ground black pepper. Put a baking sheet or aluminum foil on the bottom rack of the oven to catch any drips. Put the cast iron back in the 200°F oven for an hour or so.

• Store cast iron without a lid on it. Moisture is what causes problems. When I don't leave my skillets on the stove, I keep them in the oven.

• If you find an old rusty cast-iron piece at a garage sale, get it. Remove the rust and reseason. Better yet, if you inherit a cast-iron piece, love it and use it. Cast iron is like Southern family jewelry—it should be passed down through the generations along with all the stories about the family members who used it.

- Use any utensils you want with the cast iron—metal spoons, wooden spoons, a whisk, whatever. This is not a fussy surface. I would never use a pan that doesn't have multiple purposes. Who has the time to remember what goes with what, or the room to store specialty implements? I keep all my utensils on my counter and my skillets on the stove and use them interchangeably.

- As long as you regularly use your cast iron, you will rarely need to reseason. If it's been a while since you've used yours and you want to freshen it a little but you don't need to reseason, sauté some garlic and chopped onions in it to get it back into shape. Do be warned that the smell will inevitably create a craving for something savory and delicious.

BACON AND DRIPPINS

I keep a pickle jar of bacon drippins on my kitchen counter at all times. Bacon drippins is another versatile ingredient, and one of my staples. When something calls for fat, whether it's butter or oil, bacon drippins is another option to try. It gives a different dimension to the dishes you may have always used butter or oil for, and it keeps in a jar, unrefrigerated, for months. You'll know it's turned bad when it loses its texture and looks more like cottage cheese.

In this chapter, a few of the recipes include frying the bacon in a skillet, removing the bacon, and using the remaining drippins to cook the other ingredients. That method works great, but when you need more bacon for a crowd or you're in a hurry and can't stand over the stove, you can cook your bacon in the oven instead.

- When I fix bacon in the oven, I cook it in my largest skillet or on a baking sheet with sides.

- I cook the bacon at 400°F for 15 to 18 minutes without flipping, making sure to keep the oven shut the whole time.

- If you're cooking something and need your oven to be set at 350°F, you can cook the bacon in the oven for 25 minutes.

- To collect the drippins once you've removed the bacon, pour the grease into a glass jar, set in the sink just in case any spills. If you are averse to the brown bits in the drippins, you can put a strainer or small colander over the opening of the jar. But I leave the brown bits in. That's where the flavor is.

- I add a little drippins to veggies for roasting, my cornbread batter, a dollop when I'm cooking rice. Everything in moderation, as they say: A little drippins adds just that scrumptious something, and a touch goes a long way. Experiment with it and pretty soon you'll know the amount of drippins you like melted over your green beans or even tossed in pasta with fresh vegetables.

Frying Frying can be a mess, but in my opinion it's well worth it. It can also make your house smell like fried food, but I can think of worse things for a house to smell like. One way to avoid both of these impediments, however, is a method I mention in the recipe for Lemon Zest Cast-Iron Fried Shrimp (page 58): frying outside. Many grills have burners on the side, and this is a great place to do your frying. You can also use a propane burner outside.

Keeping the oil—and I usually use peanut oil—at a consistent temperature of 350°F is the most important thing to get right when frying. A high-quality digital thermometer with a probe is invaluable in this case. Once you put the chicken or other food in the oil, the temperature is going to drop. Using your thermometer as a guide, adjust the burner accordingly to keep the temperature stabilized at 350°F, and then continue to adjust as needed.

AUNT MARTHA'S BISCUIT DOUGHNUTS

When I was growing up, my father was a single dad, and I spent a lot of time at my Uncle Larry and Aunt Martha's. Aunt Martha had children close to my age and we would play together, and I would enjoy the fact that at Aunt Martha's we were allowed to run a little more wild and free than I was used to and eat whatever we wanted, including Lucky Charms and Mountain Dew. On Saturday mornings, Aunt Martha would plug in a Fry Daddy and we would use the Mountain Dew bottle caps to punch holes in canned biscuits to make homemade doughnuts. Then we got to cover the doughnuts in powdered sugar or cinnamon sugar. It was a child's absolute delight. I loved sharing this activity when we visited our friends the Ulmers in Jackson, Wyoming. I think it's earned me "favorite adult" status among the Ulmer children.

Makes 10 each, doughnuts and holes

1 tube refrigerated regular
   biscuit dough (not jumbo)
¼ cup white sugar
1 teaspoon ground cinnamon
Vegetable oil, for frying
Garnish (optional): Powdered
   sugar, colored sprinkles

1 Use a bottle cap to cut out the center of the biscuits. Reserve the centers to cook as doughnut holes. Combine the white sugar and cinnamon and set aside.
2 In a deep, heavy pot or deep skillet, heat to 350°F enough vegetable oil to cover the biscuits.
3 Add a few biscuits at a time and fry until golden brown,

45 seconds to 1 minute per side. Remove with a wire mesh strainer and drain on a paper bag. Fry the doughnut biscuits and "holes."
4 While the doughnuts are still warm, toss with the cinnamon sugar, or with powdered sugar or sprinkles if you wish.

PIMENTO CHEESE
SHRIMP AND GRITS

Shrimp and grits has become synonymous with Lowcountry cuisine, and when I meet people from elsewhere, they always want to know my take on it. I put this recipe together one Father's Day for my dad, a Lowcountry boy who loves his shrimp. In fact, Magwood's, the only place I go for fresh local shrimp, is located on Shem Creek within walking distance of my father's house, where I grew up. I would ride my bike along the oak-shaded streets and out to the water's edge to watch the pelicans, sea gulls, and dolphins dive behind the incoming shrimp boats as the shrimpers swept out the bycatch. When that's part of your childhood, it's hard to ever buy anything other than fresh shrimp right off the docks. My Lowcountry-raised friend Krysten, who now lives in California, has her parents send her fresh Shem Creek shrimp via overnight delivery. Any other shrimp just isn't the same. Come down here and try it. You'll see what I mean.

Instead of covering up the taste of the fresh shrimp with too many fussy ingredients, this version uses the onion and garlic to enhance the taste of the shrimp, with the fresh tomatoes brightening up the whole dish. And, of course, a little bacon drippins never hurts. Forget the smell of cookies baking—to me there's nothing better than the smell of garlic and onions cooking in bacon drippins on the stove or roasting in the oven. Enjoy the smell of this recipe in the kitchen and enjoy how the shrimp take on those same flavors. Just be sure not to overcook the shrimp—that's what gives them a tough or chewy texture.

Makes 4 servings

4 servings grits (see Note)
4 tablespoons (½ stick) butter, at room temperature
½ cup homemade or *high-quality* purchased pimento cheese (hint hint)

½ pound sliced bacon
1 pint cherry tomatoes, cut in half
1 large onion, diced (about 1 cup)
4 cloves garlic, minced
1½ pounds shrimp, rinsed, peeled, and deveined

Kosher salt and freshly ground black pepper
½ cup shredded sharp cheddar cheese
3 green onions, thinly sliced (white and green parts)

1 Preheat the oven to 400°F.
2 Make the grits. In the last 5 minutes of cooking, stir in the butter and pimento cheese. Keep warm.
3 Cook the bacon in a large skillet. Remove from the pan, drain on a paper bag, crumble, and set aside.
4 Drain off and set aside half the bacon drippins from the skillet (about 2 tablespoons), and add the tomatoes, onion, and garlic to the remaining drippins. Cook on medium-high heat for 1 to 2 minutes, then place in the oven for 15 to 20 minutes, shaking the pan halfway through.
5 Spoon out the tomatoes and set aside to keep warm. Pour the reserved bacon drippins into the pan, add the shrimp, and cook on medium heat for 2 minutes, until just pink.
6 Turn the shrimp and return the tomatoes to pan. Cook a minute or two, until cooked through. Taste and season with salt and pepper.
7 Spoon the shrimp and tomatoes over the grits. Top with the cheddar cheese, crumbled bacon, and green onions.

Note: When cooking the grits, use the measure of liquid to grits recommended on the package, but use milk instead of water. For more on grits, see page 82.

CAST-IRON PARTY SHRIMP

My mother adapted this from a Paul Prudhomme recipe and taught it to me, and it was one of the first things I fixed for friends when I was living on my own and just starting to have people over. This dish is served right out of the skillet with warm bread, and it blends Southern and French flavors: the skillet and shrimp on one hand and the French bread and stock on the other. It's so easy, yet somehow it feels sophisticated to have everyone gathered around, eating right from the skillet with their bread sopping up the liquid, very European with an effortless sort of elegance. Skillets are considered no-nonsense workhorses in the kitchen, but their versatility and simple design makes them immanently stylish and table worthy.

Makes 8 servings

DRY SEASONING MIX
2 teaspoons cayenne pepper
2 teaspoons freshly ground black pepper
1 teaspoon kosher salt
1 teaspoon crushed red pepper flakes

1 teaspoon dried rosemary leaves, crushed
¾ teaspoon dried thyme
½ teaspoon dried oregano

4 dozen medium-large shell-on shrimp (about 2 pounds)

½ pound (2 sticks) plus 2 to 4 tablespoons butter
2 to 3 teaspoons minced garlic
2 teaspoons Worcestershire sauce
1 cup shrimp stock or chicken stock
¾ cup beer, at room temperature
French baguettes, warmed

1 Make the dry seasoning mix: Combine all the ingredients.
2 Rinse the shrimp and drain well.
3 Melt the ½ pound butter in a cast-iron or other large, heavy skillet. Add the garlic, Worcestershire, and seasoning mix. Add the shrimp. Do not stir, but shake the pan back and forth for about 3 minutes.
4 Add the remaining 2 to 4 tablespoons butter (or to taste or preference) and stock and cook 2 minutes. Add the beer and cook 1 minute. Remove from the heat and let rest for 3 minutes.
5 Swish the shrimp in the pan sauce and serve with warmed baguettes.

My California-born husband claims not to like fried food. Please. He gobbles up these pork chops every time, and when I've gone awhile without making them, he makes sure to head to one of our favorite local restaurants where on Tuesdays the special is pork chops. The lunch plate comes with two chops, and he eats one at lunch and brings the other one home. I'd like to think he eats the one and brings the other home to share with me, but that's never the case. He inhales it before I even have a chance—every time.

This particular recipe is one of my personal masterpieces (in my opinion), and it was created out of pure desperation. I'd hosted an oyster roast the night before, and let's say I was feeling just a little bit peaked from the hostessing duties, and the only cure was fried pork chops. All the meat-and-threes were closed on Sunday, and we were completely out of flour because I'd made a bunch of biscuits a few days before. All we had that I could think of using for breading was the saltine crackers left over from serving the oysters the night before. They say necessity is the mother of invention, and she did not let me down on this one!

Makes 4 servings

4 bone-in 1-inch-thick pork chops
1½ teaspoons kosher salt
¾ teaspoon freshly ground black pepper
1 sleeve saltine crackers
1 tablespoon minced fresh sage
1 tablespoon minced fresh thyme
2 cups grated Parmesan cheese
2 large eggs
Vegetable oil, for frying
4 cloves garlic, cut in half
4 green onions, thinly sliced (white and green parts)

1 Season the pork chops with 1 teaspoon of the salt and ½ teaspoon of the pepper.
2 Place the saltines in a resealable plastic bag and use a rolling pin to crush them. Add the sage, thyme, and the remaining ¼ teaspoon pepper.
3 Set up a breading station with three shallow bowls: Put the cheese in one. Beat the eggs with the remaining ½ teaspoon salt in the second. Pour the saltine crumbs into the third. Set up one cooling rack over waxed paper and another over a baking sheet.
4 Coat the pork chops in the cheese, then the eggs (allow the excess egg to drip back into the bowl), and finally the saltines. Place the chops on the rack over the waxed paper and allow to set for 8 to 10 minutes.
5 Heat a cast-iron skillet on medium-high heat. Pour in enough oil to come up ¼ inch. Add the garlic and cook 3 minutes, or until fragrant. Remove and discard the garlic. Add the chops and fry for 4 minutes per side, until crisp and brown on the outside and barely pink on the inside.
6 Remove to the clean rack to drain briefly. Serve topped with the green onions.

KITCHEN SINK PAN-FRIED
PORK CHOPS

CAST-IRON HERB LAMB CHOPS

One Easter I was set to host my in-laws, and I wanted something that reflected the welcome spring flavors, something with a Mediterranean feel. Something that wasn't pork. I was dying to use my fresh herbs that had just started to flourish with the warmer weather. So I settled on lamb chops. The versatility of the cast-iron skillet allows you to use this same method on almost any meat: Marinate, sear, and finish in the oven for a great crust with a moist inside. I've since made these countless times, sometimes as a meal and sometimes with little rib chops as an elegant appetizer for a party. Elegant, that is, until you catch your guests gnawing the bones bare and licking their fingers to get as much of this delectable flavor as possible. And you won't blame them one bit.

If your garden herbs aren't ready yet, you can buy them at the grocery store. You'll make more herb paste than you need for the chops; store the extra in the fridge and use within the next day or so (or put in an ice cube tray and keep in the freezer for up to a month, popping out cubes of paste as needed).

Makes 6 servings

½ cup pine nuts
1 (1-ounce package) fresh rosemary
1 (1-ounce package) fresh mint
1 (1-ounce package) fresh basil

3 cloves garlic, coarsely chopped
½ cup chopped green onions (about 4 onions, white and green parts)
½ teaspoon kosher salt

¼ teaspoon freshly ground black pepper
¼ to ½ cup olive oil
6 lamb rib chops
½ cup crumbled feta cheese

1 Toast the pine nuts in a 325°F oven or in a skillet on the stovetop, shaking the pan every 2 minutes until the nuts are golden brown. Let cool.
2 Rinse and dry the rosemary, mint, and basil and pull the leaves off the stems. Discard the stems. Place the nuts, herbs, garlic, green onions, salt, and pepper in a food processor or blender. Pulse until finely chopped, then slowly add the olive oil until a chunky paste forms. Reserve half of the paste for another use.
3 Place the chops in a resealable plastic bag and pour in the paste. Massage the paste into the chops. Seal the bag and refrigerate 2 hours or overnight.
4 Preheat the oven to 400°F. Heat a cast-iron skillet until hot.

5 Sear the chops 2 to 3 minutes per side. Place the skillet in the oven for 4 to 6 minutes for medium rare, 6 to 8 minutes for medium.
6 Turn on the broiler. Top the chops with the feta and broil about 2 minutes to melt the cheese.

My mother has always said that along with her mother, her grandmother Mimie, great-grandmother Munner, and great-aunt Tattie all had an equal hand in raising her. She called them her "three mothers" or her "Munners," and their mothering and guidance lives on. For example, I often call my mother to discuss dinner when I need a little inspiration, and one night I had a craving for salmon. Callie told me that her Munners always loved to eat canned salmon over grits, and it had been one of her favorite meals growing up. So I decided to try fixing it with fresh salmon, and then I added okra—my favorite vegetable—cooked just like my mother had taught me. The creamy grits with the crispy okra and the hint of bitter from the arugula proved the perfect complements to the savory salmon. I think the Munners would approve.

Makes 4 servings

2 tablespoons mayonnaise
1 teaspoon Dijon mustard
1 teaspoon whole-grain mustard
1 clove garlic, minced (about ½ teaspoon)
Juice of ½ lemon
1 pound salmon fillet (1-inch-thick)

GRITS
2 cups chicken stock
2 cups water
1 cup grits (not instant or quick)
1 tablespoon butter
1 teaspoon kosher salt
½ cup whipping cream

OKRA
1 pound okra, trimmed and chopped
1 small white onion, chopped
3 pinches cayenne pepper
½ teaspoon kosher salt
¼ teaspoon freshly ground black pepper
1 tablespoon butter
1 tablespoon plus 1 teaspoon olive oil
Serving suggestion: Baby arugula

1 Combine the mayonnaise, mustards, garlic, and lemon juice. Smear over the salmon. Place in a resealable plastic bag and refrigerate for 20 minutes at a minimum or overnight. (For best results, plan to marinate overnight.)
2 Make the grits: Combine the stock and water in a saucepan and bring to a boil. Add the grits, stirring with a whisk. Reduce the heat to a low simmer and cook 20 to 30 minutes, stirring occasionally, until thick and creamy.
3 Stir in the butter, salt, and cream and cook 3 to 5 minutes more. Set aside, keeping warm.
4 Make the okra: Mix together the okra, onion, cayenne, salt, and pepper in a bowl and let sit for a few minutes for the flavors to marry.
5 Melt the butter into the 1 tablespoon olive oil in a cast-iron skillet on medium to high heat. Add the okra-onion mixture and spread in a single layer; do not overcrowd. (You will probably need to cook the okra in two batches unless you are using a large skillet.) Let the okra cook undisturbed for about 10 minutes.
6 Turn the okra to brown the other side, about 10 minutes more. (The key to fried okra is to not stir or fuss with it, so it gets crispy.) Once the okra is brown and crisp, remove to a paper bag to remove the excess grease. Keep warm.
7 When you're ready to serve, heat a cast-iron grill pan over medium-high heat and brush with the 1 teaspoon olive oil. Cook the salmon on the first side for 5 minutes. Turn and cook on the other side for 3 to 5 minutes.
8 To serve, divide the salmon into portions. Place the grits on plates. Place the salmon over the grits and serve with the okra with arugula alongside.

BEES'S EASTER EGG ORNAMENTS

The Easter we hosted my in-laws and enjoyed our Mediterranean-inspired lamb chops, my mother-in-law, Barbara—called "Bees" by my girls—shared a new Easter tradition with us. She showed us how to poke a hole at both ends of an uncooked egg with a needle, blow out the yolk and white, and then paint the delicate shell with watercolors. These eggs became instant Easter treasures that we store wrapped in newspaper in a Tupperware container and bring out every Easter. We remember that special time with Bees on the porch each time we unpack the eggs. If you try this at home, save the raw egg that comes out of the shell and make a post-decorating frittata the children will love. Food just tastes better when arts and crafts and Beeses are involved.

ROCKVILLE EASTER TRADITION

Another family Easter tradition is going over to my Aunt Gail and Uncle Jimmy's. Not only do they put on a delicious traditional Easter meal of ham and red rice for their children and grandchildren and their siblings and *their* children and grandchildren, but Easters at their home in Rockville, South Carolina, are special for so many other reasons as well. Their house is right on the river, and the oak trees are so large that the eggs for the egg hunt are hidden among the roots and branches of only one giant tree. After lunch, the adults enjoy a game of "tree golf." There are eighteen trees spread across the property. Each adult gets a beer, a club, and a ball. The goal is to hit each tree with the ball—as opposed to putting the ball into a hole. Walking an eighteen-hole golf course was never so enjoyable, even though our aim does tend to get a little worse as the afternoon wears on. I don't think real golf could ever appeal to me now—tree golf at Aunt Gail and Uncle Jimmy's has ruined me.

GRITCAKES WITH
SKILLET-SEARED SAUSAGE

What to do with leftover grits? Gritcakes! This is a delicious weeknight meal that I can easily cobble together using ingredients left from previous meals and staples that I always keep on hand. Whenever I see smoked sausage on sale, I get two and put one in the freezer. And whenever I have leftover cooked grits, I throw them in the fridge or freezer as well, in a 20-ounce rectangular plastic container so they form a ½-inch-thick layer. This way, I almost always have everything I need to make one of my favorite and most delicious throw-together suppers. The silky skillet juices with the crunchy gritcakes make a fabulous texture combination of crispiness and gooeyness. I have to remind myself to eat slowly. . . .

Makes 4 servings

3 tablespoons vegetable oil
1 large white onion, cut in half and sliced thin
1 green bell pepper, seeded and thinly sliced
2 red bell peppers, seeded and thinly sliced
2 cloves garlic, minced

1 pound kielbasa or other smoked sausage, sliced
1 cup chicken broth
2 tablespoons butter

GRITCAKES
Leftover grits (thawed if frozen), at room temperature

1 cup homemade or panko breadcrumbs
¼ cup grated Parmesan cheese
2 teaspoons kosher salt
1 teaspoon freshly ground black pepper
2 tablespoons vegetable oil

1 Heat 2 tablespoons of the vegetable oil in a large skillet on medium heat. Add the onion and peppers and cook until almost soft, 10 to 13 minutes.
2 Add the garlic and cook for 2 minutes more. Remove the vegetables from the pan and reserve.
3 Pour the remaining 1 tablespoon oil into the skillet and add the sausage. Cook until browned well on both sides, 8 to 10 minutes.

4 Add the broth, bring to a boil, and scrape up any browned bits. Add back the vegetables and melt in the butter. Keep warm.
5 Make the gritcakes: Put a cooking rack over a baking sheet and place in the oven. Preheat the oven to 300°F. Cut the grits into 8 (½-inch-thick) slices. Combine the breadcrumbs, cheese, salt, and pepper in a shallow bowl or dish. Dip the grits slices in the breadcrumbs, patting to adhere

the breadcrumbs onto the slices. Heat the oil in a skillet on high heat. Working in batches, add a few of the gritcakes and cook 2 to 4 minutes per side, until golden brown and crunchy. Do not crowd the pan. Remove the gritcakes to the cooking rack to keep hot as you cook the rest.
6 To serve, top the gritcakes with the smoked sausage, onion, peppers, and pan gravy.

LEMON ZEST CAST-IRON
FRIED SHRIMP

Friday night is steak night at our house. So what does that have to do with fried shrimp? Well, by Friday night I'm ready to kick back and relax. Cooking steak on the grill outside, sitting on the back porch with family and friends, having a glass of wine, watching dusk descend on the marsh, there's really nothing better.

My oldest child, Caroline, had been craving fried shrimp one particular week. My father, stepmother, and brother Alston were coming over that Friday. Alston loves coming over to our house because our backyard is right on the Ashley River, and he loves being by the water and the marsh. He also loves fried shrimp. So I promised to do shrimp and steak. The only problem was that once the grill was getting hot, I really didn't feel like leaving the party to go inside the kitchen to fry shrimp. But Caroline and Alston were watching my every move, ready for the shrimp I couldn't cook fast enough, in their opinion. So

I said, "Hell, I'll just fry them out here." And so Lemon Zest Cast-Iron Fried Shrimp ended up adding a whole new element to my repertoire—frying outside.

My grill has an extra burner on the side, which is as easy as frying inside—without the mess or the fry smell. You can also fry right on the grill. The trick with frying right on the grill is keeping the temperature even, and it is tricky because adjustments take longer than with a burner. Use your digital thermometer diligently to help. But if you do have that extra burner, start using it and enjoy your own party. A woman at the grill with tongs in one hand, a glass of wine in the other, and steak and shrimp sizzling before her with all the smells and smoke that entails is one hot image to behold, according to my husband. Try it!

Makes 4 servings

---

1 pound large shrimp (20 to 25 count)

MARINADE
Grated zest of 1 lemon
1 cup buttermilk
1½ teaspoons kosher salt

½ teaspoon freshly ground black pepper
Juice of ½ lemon
1 teaspoon hot sauce, or more to taste

1 large egg
2 teaspoons kosher salt
¾ cup all-purpose flour
1 teaspoon freshly ground black pepper
½ cup vegetable oil
Tartar Sauce (recipe follows)

---

1 Peel, devein, and rinse the shrimp. Place in a colander to drain.
2 Make the marinade: Set aside ½ teaspoon of the lemon zest for the shrimp coating. In a resealable plastic bag, combine

the remaining zest, the buttermilk, salt, pepper, juice, and hot sauce. Mix well. Add the shrimp and seal the bag. Refrigerate for 30 minutes at a minimum or overnight. (For best results, plan to marinate overnight.)

3 Set up a coating station with two shallow bowls: In one bowl, beat the egg with ½ teaspoon of the salt. Combine the flour with the remaining 1½ teaspoons salt, the pepper, and the reserved ½ teaspoon lemon zest in the other bowl. Place a cooling rack over waxed paper.

4 Drain the shrimp and discard the marinade. Dip the shrimp in the egg, then toss in the seasoned flour to coat. Place on the cooling rack to set while the oil heats.

5 Pour the vegetable oil into a cast-iron skillet and heat to 350°F. Fry the shrimp 2 minutes on one side; turn and fry 1 minute longer. Remove to a paper bag to drain briefly. Serve with tartar sauce.

Tartar Sauce

Makes about 1½ cups

½ cup mayonnaise
½ cup sour cream
¼ cup chopped green onions (about 2 onions, white and green parts)
¼ cup minced kosher dill pickles
1 tablespoon minced fresh flat-leaf parsley
1 clove garlic, minced
½ teaspoon grated lemon zest
½ teaspoon hot sauce, or more to taste
½ teaspoon Dijon mustard
½ teaspoon kosher salt

Combine all the ingredients. Chill at least 30 minutes for the flavors to marry.

MRS. BURNS AND AMY'S
COUNTRY FRIED STEAK

Amy Burns is one of my best friends. We became instant friends when we met playing basketball against each other in high school. She was like a sister to me right from the start. We lived across town from each other—"across the bridge"—which in those days felt like a great distance. I'd often spend the night at her house, even on weeknights. Amy's mother, Madeline, is an incredible cook, and their family has always been so close. Every night the whole family sat down to eat supper together. Living with my father and stepmother who both worked, I was accustomed to sitting down to a family meal on Sundays only. So the whole concept of a nightly sit-down meal with the family was foreign to me.

Not only that, but Mrs. Burns had a calendar with every meal planned for every night of the whole month. Our friend Krysten and I thought this calendar was the craziest thing we'd ever seen, and we loved to laugh about it. And yet . . . Krysten and I would regularly check the calendar on the Burnses' refrigerator for our favorite meals so we would know which days we wanted to ask if we could come over. The meal I always searched for was Mrs. Burns's country fried steak. I will never forget the way the Burnses welcomed me to their family table. And I will never forget how out-of-this-world good Mrs. Burns's country fried steak was. Now Amy makes it for her young family. She even has her own monthly food calendar. Her children's friends will love her for it!

Mrs. Burns and Amy serve this with mashed potatoes or rice, but that might just put me over the edge of indulgence! I usually serve it sprinkled with chopped green onions and with an arugula salad on the side.

Makes 6 servings

1 cup all-purpose flour
Kosher salt and freshly ground
    black pepper
½ teaspoon cayenne pepper
½ teaspoon dry mustard
½ teaspoon minced fresh thyme
6 thin cube steaks
1 cup vegetable oil
1 cup beef stock
1 tablespoon butter

1 Combine the flour with 1½ teaspoons salt, 1½ teaspoons pepper, the cayenne, mustard, and thyme. Dredge the steaks in the seasoned flour. Place the steaks on a cooling rack and allow to set about 30 minutes. Save ¼ cup of the seasoned flour for the gravy. **2** In a cast-iron skillet, heat the oil to 350°F. Cook the steaks for 2 minutes per side. Remove the steaks to a paper bag to drain. Keep warm while you make the gravy. **3** Spoon out all but ¼ cup of the drippins from the pan. (Be sure to leave the good browned bits.) Whisk in the reserved flour and cook on medium-high heat for about 5 minutes, until crispy. **4** Whisk in the beef stock and cook until bubbling and thickened. Melt in the butter. Taste and adjust the salt and pepper. **5** Serve the steaks with the gravy.

VEGETABLE GRATIN

Mama used to make the yummiest vegetable casserole, and I would gobble it up. (She baked it in a casserole dish instead of a skillet, but thinking about Mama for this chapter reminded me of it, and I didn't want to leave it out.) Even though "vegetable casserole" sounded healthy, in hindsight it's no wonder that all of us grandchildren had no problem cleaning our plates of it. I'm pretty sure it was a few cans of Veg-All mixed with cans of creamy condensed soup and topped with butter and Ritz crackers. So in honor of Mama's original, I concocted a healthier version that my children gobble up. In fact, it's such a hearty dish, I often pair it with some good bread and serve it as a meal in itself. You can vary and experiment with the type of vegetables. You can even switch out the breadcrumbs for buttered Ritz when you feel the hankering for a little bit of old-school kitchen-table comfort food. Ritz or no Ritz, within 10 minutes of putting this casserole in the oven your entire house will smell amazing.

Makes 6 servings

---

1 pint cherry tomatoes, cut in half
¾ pound cauliflower, chopped
¾ pound yellow squash, chopped
¾ pound zucchini, chopped
5 cloves garlic, minced

¼ cup olive oil
1 teaspoon kosher salt
½ teaspoon freshly ground black pepper
½ cup grated Parmesan cheese, plus more for topping

Butter for casserole dish
6 tablespoons (¾ stick) butter, melted
1 cup panko breadcrumbs

---

1 Combine the tomatoes, cauliflower, yellow squash, zucchini, and garlic in a large bowl. Add the olive oil, salt, pepper, and Parmesan cheese and mix well. Let sit 1 hour for the flavors to marry.

2 Preheat the oven to 400°F. Butter a casserole or gratin dish large enough for everything to fit.
3 Transfer the vegetables to the casserole. Top with the breadcrumbs, drizzle with the melted butter, and sprinkle with more cheese.
4 Bake 35 to 45 minutes; cover the top with foil if looks like it's browning too quickly.
5 Remove from the oven and let set for 10 minutes before serving.

REUNION FRIED CHICKEN

I sometimes wonder if I didn't create my own undoing with this fried chicken, but I was in a high-pressure situation. My husband and I had a whirlwind romance—we got engaged only three months after we met in New York City. John's family had moved from California to Jackson, Wyoming, when he was twelve, so most of his friends and family were living in Wyoming and Idaho when we met. When we flew out to Idaho right after our engagement, it was my first time meeting his friends. Before we knew it, a going-away/engagement party was in the works. I wanted to show the Westerners what a real Southern supper was like, so I decided fried chicken was in order.

I don't think I left the kitchen the entire party. His friends had hardly met me and already John had a Southern wife sweating away in the kitchen making fried chicken while they had fun around the fire outside. If I do say so myself, at least the version of fried chicken I came up with on the fly to impress his Western friends ended up being a keeper. The only downside is that whenever I return to Idaho, the first thing people say to me is, "When're you going to make some more of that fried chicken?"

What started as an attempt to endear myself to his friends and share some Southern cooking has developed into a standing Idaho tradition for our family, hence the name Reunion Fried Chicken. We spend a good bit of time in Idaho every summer, and we go to the rodeo once a week. On the afternoon of rodeo day, while my girls are napping, I fry the chicken, put it in a paper bag, and keep it in the oven at 200°F until it's time to go. When we get to the rodeo, I have warm chicken on hand in the bag, and should anyone ask me about the fried chicken, I'm prepared.

This chicken also tastes good cold the next day, and, even though it's a little decadent, leftover fried chicken makes very tasty chicken salad.

Makes 4 servings

CHICKEN
1 whole chicken (3 to 3½ pounds)
Kosher salt and freshly ground
   black pepper

MARINADE
3 cups buttermilk
2 tablespoons light brown sugar

2 tablespoons kosher salt
2 tablespoons paprika
1 teaspoon cayenne pepper
1 teaspoon ground cinnamon

SEASONED FLOUR
2 cups all-purpose flour
1 tablespoon kosher salt

1 teaspoon paprika
½ teaspoon cayenne pepper
½ teaspoon ground cinnamon,
   or more to taste

4 large eggs
Vegetable oil, for frying

1 Cut the chicken into 10 pieces: 2 legs, 2 thighs, 2 wings, and the 2 breast halves each cut in half. Season the chicken pieces with salt and pepper and place in a large resealable plastic bag.
2 Make the marinade: Combine all the ingredients. Pour over the chicken and seal the bag. Refrigerate 4 hours or overnight.
3 Make the seasoned flour: Combine all the ingredients in a bowl. Beat the eggs in a second bowl. Set up one cooling rack over a piece of waxed paper and a second rack over a baking sheet.
4 Drain the chicken and discard the marinade. One at a time, dredge the chicken pieces in the flour, then dip to coat with the eggs, then coat with the flour again. Place the pieces on the rack and allow to set for about 10 minutes.
5 Pour oil into a cast-iron skillet to a depth of ½ inch and heat the oil to 365°F on high heat.

You want to fry at 350°F, but the temperature will go down when you add the pieces of chicken, so get it a little higher to start.
6 Fry the chicken pieces, dark meat first, skin side down first, about 8 minutes per side, or until the meat reaches an internal temperature of 165°F. Remove to the clean rack and continue frying until all the chicken is cooked.

Skillet Sides

If you've ever enrolled in a CSA (Community Sponsored Agriculture) program, which provides a weekly share of fresh produce from a local farm, you know the excited anticipation of wondering what will be in the box that week. I love that feeling, but I've also stared into the box and wondered, "What the heck am I going to do with that?" If all other inspiration fails for a vegetable you may not be familiar with, you can always clean it, cut it, put it in a cast-iron skillet, drizzle it with butter and salt, and roast it in the oven. You can even mix different vegetables and roast them together as a medley.

Below are some of my go-to veggie preparations; you can use the same methods to fix other vegetables as well. Think of them as techniques for experimenting with whatever's in your veggie box.

Any vegetable works! I've used asparagus, cauliflower, green beans, and new potatoes as examples below, but adapt this method for whatever you have. And leftovers can be used in soups or added to salads.

Makes 6 servings

NO-FAIL VEGETABLE ROASTING

1 Preheat the oven to 425°F.
2 What is important is that the vegetable pieces be of similar size: all thin asparagus or all thick asparagus, for example. Potatoes should be halved or quartered to keep pieces a consistent size.
3 Toss the vegetables with olive oil, kosher salt, and freshly ground black pepper.
4 Roast in a cast-iron skillet or other ovenproof skillet, a baking pan with sides, or a roasting pan.
5 Top the vegetables with fresh lemon juice, grated lemon zest, grated cheese, fresh herbs—or nothing other than the salt and pepper.
6 I usually open the oven door and shake the pan once during roasting, so the vegetables cook evenly and get really brown on more than one side.

Asparagus Bend asparagus stalks so the end of the stem naturally breaks off; discard the ends. Toss 2 pounds of asparagus with 3 tablespoons olive oil, 1½ teaspoons kosher salt, and freshly ground black pepper. Roast 15 to 18 minutes. Squeeze fresh lemon juice on top when they come out of the oven.

Cauliflower Separate a 2-pound head of cauliflower into same-size florets. Mix with 2 to 3 cloves of chopped garlic, 1 chopped small white onion, and olive oil. Season with salt and pepper and roast for 45 minutes, or until brown and caramelized. Top with grated Parmesan cheese.

Green beans If you wish, trim the ends from 2 pounds green beans. Toss the beans with 3 tablespoons olive oil, kosher salt, and freshly ground black pepper. Roast 18 to 20 minutes, until tender. Squeeze fresh lemon juice on them when roasted.

New potatoes Cut 2 pounds potatoes into similar sizes. Mix with 2 or 3 chopped cloves of garlic, 1 diced white onion, and 3 tablespoons olive oil. Roast until browned and crispy, 45 to 60 minutes. Fresh rosemary goes well with these potatoes.

BACON BRUSSELS SPROUTS

Makes 6 servings

4 slices bacon
½ cup chopped onion (Vidalia or other sweet onion
  preferred)
2 cloves garlic, thinly sliced
2 pounds Brussels sprouts, trimmed and cut in half
  lengthwise
Grated Parmesan cheese

1 Preheat the oven to 400°F.
2 Cook the bacon in a cast-iron skillet on low heat.
Remove the bacon, drain, and chop.
3 Add the onion, garlic, and Brussels sprouts to
the bacon drippins. Shake the pan to mix and coat
everything. Roast for 12 to 15 minutes, shaking
the pan once.
4 After you pull out the pan, add the bacon and
sprinkle with Parmesan to taste.

SPRINGTIME SUCCOTASH
WITH BACON

Makes 6 to 8 servings

4 slices bacon
1 small white onion, chopped (about ½ cup)
2 cloves garlic, finely chopped (about 1 teaspoon)
2 cups chopped tomatoes (about 2 large tomatoes)
2 cups fresh corn kernels (about 4 ears)
2 cups cooked black-eyed peas (see page 102)
Kosher salt and freshly ground black pepper
Hot sauce

1 Preheat the oven to 400°F.
2 Cook the bacon in a cast-iron skillet on medium
heat. Remove the bacon, drain, and chop.
3 Add the onion, garlic, tomatoes, corn, and black-
eyed peas to the drippins in the pan. Shake the
pan to mix and coat everything. Roast for 15 to 20
minutes.
4 Taste and season with salt and pepper. Serve
with hot sauce.

CAST-IRON GREEN BEANS
WITH SOY AND SESAME

You can use this same method to fix asparagus or snow peas. Roast 10 minutes instead of 15 to 20.

Makes 4 servings

1 pound green beans, tips removed
1 tablespoon soy sauce
1½ teaspoons sesame oil

1 Preheat the oven to 400°F.
2 Place the beans in a cast-iron skillet. Sprinkle with the soy sauce and sesame oil and toss to coat. Roast for 15 to 20 minutes, until just crispy.

NICCI'S CREAMED CORN

A quick note about this recipe: My dear friend Nicci is the one who suggested I add fresh tarragon to creamed corn. To be honest, the idea did not appeal to me, but I gave it a try and fell in love. Every once in a while I don't mind being proved wrong . . . at least in the kitchen!

Makes 4 servings

Kosher salt
5 ears corn, shucked
2 tablespoons butter
1 cup whole milk
Leaves from 4 sprigs fresh tarragon, chopped

1 Bring a large pot of salted water to a boil. Cook the corn 5 minutes. Drain, cool, and cut the kernels from the cobs.
2 Melt the butter in a cast-iron skillet on low heat. Add the corn and cook, stirring constantly, for 3 minutes.
3 Increase the heat to medium. Slowly add the milk and stir until almost all the milk is absorbed. Taste and adjust the salt. Remove from the heat and stir in the tarragon.

CAROLINE'S
MACARONI PIE

If you really want to go all out, serve this with your fried chicken. Or serve this with anything, to be honest. It's that good. I don't know why Grandmama (the "Caroline" of this recipe and one of many Carolines in the family: I'm Caroline, my mother, Callie, is Caroline, one of my daughters is Caroline, and my stepmother is Caroline!) called this macaroni "pie." There's no crust. But I think it's a Southern thing. I've had corn pie and oyster pie as well, dishes that are also cooked in the oven in a skillet or casserole dish but are something more than casseroles. This is almost like a soufflé. And to add to the mystery, this macaroni pie does not call for macaroni. It uses vermicelli or thin spaghetti instead. In Southern cooking, like Southern life, contradictions abound. This dish is a contradiction worth embracing.

I used to call Grandmama on a regular basis for reminders of how to make her macaroni pie. "Is it one cup of milk to two eggs or two cups of milk to one egg?" Once I finally had it figured out, I realized she missed my calling her to ask. I'm tempted myself to keep some of my recipes in my head rather than writing them down, just so my girls and hopefully grandchildren can call me with their desperate cooking questions one day.

You can make this to serve a ton of people. I once made enough to feed 250! It is always a crowd pleaser, and I get lots and lots of requests for this recipe. When I'm making a bunch for an event, I usually use disposable aluminum pans. I measure how much vermicelli to use by putting the uncooked noodles in each pan to get an idea of about how much to boil. Then I fill each pan three-quarters of the way full with the noodle/cheese/egg/milk mixture to leave enough room for expansion during cooking. And, of course, I top each pan with plenty of cheese.

Makes 8 servings

Kosher salt
1 pound vermicelli or thin spaghetti
4 large eggs

2 cups milk
1 teaspoon dry mustard
½ teaspoon cayenne pepper
5 cups shredded sharp cheddar cheese

2 tablespoons butter, at room temperature
Freshly ground black pepper

---

1 Bring a large pot of salted water to a boil. If baking the same day, preheat the oven to 375°F.
2 Cook the pasta for 1 minute less than the package instructions state. Drain the pasta and reserve in a little of the cooking water to cool briefly.
3 Beat together the eggs, milk, the mustard, and cayenne in a large bowl. Add the pasta and 4 cups of the cheese. Mix well.
4 Butter a 12-inch skillet with 1 tablespoon of the butter. Pour in the pasta. Top with the remaining 1 cup cheese, dot with the remaining 1 tablespoon butter, and sprinkle with salt and pepper. At this point you can cover the pie with plastic wrap and refrigerate overnight. Uncover and let the pie come up to room temperature as the oven heats to 375°F.
5 Bake 45 minutes, checking at 35 minutes, until golden brown and bubbly.

CAST-IRON
FRENCH BREAD CROUTONS

You can freeze the bread and when you're ready to use it, microwave for about 30 seconds to soften before cutting it into cubes.

Makes 3 to 4 cups croutons

1 whole-wheat French baguette, cut in ½-inch cubes
½ cup grated Parmesan cheese
Kosher salt and freshly ground black pepper
4 tablespoons (½ stick) butter
2 or 3 cloves garlic, minced
1 small onion, finely diced

1 Preheat the oven to 400°F.
2 Put the bread cubes in a bowl and add the Parmesan. Season with salt and pepper and mix well.
3 Melt the butter in a cast-iron skillet on low heat. Add the garlic and onion. Cook 5 to 7 minutes, stirring, until brown and crisp. Stir in the bread cubes and cheese. Transfer to the oven and bake until crisp, about 15 minutes. Begin to check at 12 minutes.
4 Serve warm on soups or cool to use on salads. You can store leftovers, once cool, up to 3 days in a tightly closed container.

ROASTING AND SLOW COOKING

When I was living on my own in a tiny apartment in New York City, I'd stave off homesickness by putting garlic, onions, and olive oil in aluminum foil and roasting the vegetables in the oven. I didn't even cook with them. I simply wanted the smell and comfort of home, of slow, home-cooked goodness.

Even though that apartment seems worlds away and eons ago, that smell still holds magic for me. Now I love standing in my (much larger!) kitchen in the morning, chopping onions and carrots, thinking about my day ahead and anticipating the smells that will fill the house by the day's end. But the beauty of roasting and slow cooking is that even though they may require initial chopping or searing, most of the time the prep work is minimal and the cooking goes on hands-free while you work or do whatever you need to do. There is nothing like that sensation of being away from the house and then opening your own front door on your return and being greeted by the aroma of food that's been slowly transforming itself from chopped vegetables and a piece of meat into heavenly, soulful food your family is going to love.

Roasting is part of my weekly routine. I go into deep detail in this chapter on the topic of "roasting the bird." Roasted chicken is easy to master. It's versatile. You can enjoy it on its own or you can roast a couple at a time and use the meat to make other dishes for the rest of the week. Southerners have always had a way of making the most of inexpensive ingredients, and roasted chicken is a great example of starting with a cheap piece of meat, making it taste amazing, and stretching it out to maximize its value.

The simmering and sitting that a lot of the recipes in this chapter require also fit our Southern lifestyle of casual gatherings and impromptu visits—especially when the weather turns cooler. In our family, the fall means sticking closer to home, taking it easy, playing cards and board games, and watching football. Lots of football. And all along, there's a flurry of friends and family coming and going. You never know who is going to drop by when. This drives some of my West Coast in-laws crazy. In the South, people don't call first. They just come by.

ON-HAND ESSENTIALS FOR COME-BY-AND-SEE-US DAYS

When we in the South say "Come by and see us," we mean it. No need to call first or schedule a time. If we're home, we'd love to see you. There are a few items I always have on hand for these days so that when people drop in, I'm prepared.

- Small cocktail plates—not fancy, just something easy to pop into the dishwasher
- Linen napkins (or plain cotton)—same as above, no need to be fancy; these go in the washing machine
- For one-dish meals, I pull out a stack of my favorite wide, shallow bowls my mother brought me back from Italy—they work beautifully for soups, grits, beans and rice, and salads
- Cookies

- Cooler full of cold beer
- Bloody Mary mix
- Celery sticks, sliced lemons and limes
- Freshly squeezed juices
- Vodka
- Biscuits (mais oui)
- Pimento cheese (mais oui aussi)
- Crackers (I like water crackers)

And my husband's must-have for such days: onion dip

Our friends know they have an open invitation to our house, especially on football Saturdays. We might still be in our pajamas when they get here, but we don't mind. We'll put together some Bloody Marys and stick some more biscuits in the oven. Throughout the day, snacks and drinks come out of the kitchen, and people come and go, some just for a quick beer, while some stay and sit all day. Whoever's lucky enough to be there late in the afternoon can enjoy whatever I've had cooking, whether it's pulled pork BBQ or beef stew, grits topped with bacon and cheese, or a couple of roasted birds.

What I love about this setup is that with the prep work done ahead of time I get to enjoy myself instead of working in the kitchen preparing food as people arrive. Almost all of these recipes serve a crowd and keep well, so there's no need to try to anticipate how many people you'll be feeding. A lot of these recipes can serve as a one-dish meal, and people can serve themselves at their leisure. I love throwing fancy parties every now and then, but I also love opening my home to my friends and treating them like family: "Go on into the kitchen and fix a plate!" And when I share my home and what's been cooking all day in my kitchen, I hope I can pass along the same sense of family togetherness and comfort that I've always cherished. And I hope my friends and family are as thankful as I am that I got to where my garlic and onions have gone from being air freshener to food.

HOMEMADE FRENCH ONION DIP

Makes about 2 cups

4 tablespoons (½ stick) butter
2 teaspoons vegetable oil
2 cups diced yellow onions
3 cloves garlic, minced
3 dashes Worcestershire sauce

1 (8-ounce) container sour cream
½ cup mayonnaise
Kosher salt and freshly ground
   black pepper

SERVING SUGGESTIONS
Chopped green onions
Potato chips
Carrots
Celery sticks
Pretzels

1 Melt the butter into the oil in a saucepan on medium-low heat. When hot and bubbling, add the onions. Cook slowly, adding the garlic after 5 minutes. Cook 20 to 30 minutes more to caramelize the onions to golden brown.

2 Stir in the Worcestershire. Remove the onions to a bowl and let cool.
3 Stir in the sour cream and mayonnaise. Cover and refrigerate for the flavors to marry.

4 Before serving, taste and season with salt and pepper.

Note: For special occasions, whip this dip!

CARRIE'S TIPS

Roasted chicken was a supper I moaned and groaned over as a teenager. My father and wonderful stepmother, Caroline, both worked, and I was often busy myself during the week playing sports, leaving Sunday as our only day for a sit-down meal. And every Sunday it was the same thing: roasted chicken. One year I even gave up chicken for Lent as an attempt to avoid eating it for a few weeks. Now, however, roasted chicken is my ultimate comfort food, and I fix it at least once a week. My girls could practically fix it themselves, they've helped me prepare it so many times. I think I've nearly perfected my method—the crust, the flavor, the moistness, all make it supremely tasty. But I don't think my method is why I crave it or why I get a feeling of satisfaction and peace as I arrange a "nest" for it in the pan. I think it's because of Caroline.

Maybe at the time, in my teenage tendency to dislike everything my parents did and said, I wasn't blown away by the food she fixed. But somehow, in my psyche, the way Caroline brought us together as a family to gather around the table became associated with her chicken. Now every time I prepare roasted chicken, I may not be thinking specifically about those Sunday chicken dinners, but I'm carrying on and appreciating that sense of family togetherness and love that Caroline brought to the table in a predictable way that I didn't even know I needed. When a friend has a baby, I always take over a roasted

chicken and some buttermilk biscuits. It really is a meal from my heart.

My girls call roasted chicken "the bird," and once you've gotten down pat the general technique for roasting it, you can use the bird as a blank slate for all kinds of variations in flavor and toppings. You can even make pan gravy to serve over rice. You may find that the bird becomes your weekly craving as well.

Dress the bird. The basic method for prepping the bird is to squeeze one-half of a lemon over the outside and then put the other half inside the cavity. Next, slather olive oil all over the outside. Sprinkle with generous amounts of kosher salt and freshly ground black pepper. If possible, dress the bird the day before and refrigerate it overnight. The next day, pull it out and let it get to room temperature, usually an hour or so, before roasting.

Make a nest. The bird needs a home. This can be a large cast-iron skillet, a roasting pan, or even a glass casserole dish. In the middle, build a nest for the bird. The simplest nest consists of 1 cup each of coarsely chopped carrots, celery, and onion, plus 2 garlic cloves (cut in half), all tossed with olive oil and salt and pepper. Arrange the pieces in the shape of a nest and sprinkle with salt and pepper and a teaspoon of olive oil. Perch the bird on top, breast up. You can also add potatoes or other vegetables around the nest to serve with the bird.
Add variety (if you're in the mood).

- Garlic: Put whole cloves of garlic in the cavity, rub garlic under the skin of the chicken, or add more garlic to the nest.

- Greek: Squeeze 2 lemons over the entire chicken and put one of the squeezed lemons inside the cavity. After slathering the olive oil on the chicken, add a generous amount of fresh oregano. After removing the chicken from the oven, squeeze another lemon over the chicken and vegetables before serving.

- Dijon: Mix 1 tablespoon Dijon mustard with 2 minced garlic cloves, 1 teaspoon chopped fresh thyme, and 1 tablespoon olive oil and rub all over the chicken after you've squeezed lemon over it and salted and peppered it.

- BBQ: Use lemon, lime, or orange when dressing this one. Cover the bird with your favorite BBQ sauce after dressing it, saving a little sauce to serve at the table. (See page 225 for my BBQ sauce recipe.)

Roast it. Make sure the bird is at room temperature. Pour ½ cup chicken stock into the pan. Roast in a 375°F oven for 1 hour and 20 to 1 hour and 30 minutes, until the juices run clear or until a digital thermometer inserted into the thigh registers 160°F.

Rest it. Let the bird sit for 5 to 10 minutes before serving.

Heat the veggies. If you included potatoes or you'd like to eat the veggies in the nest, after you remove the chicken, turn the oven up to 400°F and roast the veggies in the pan for a few minutes, until they are browned and a little crisp on top.

Make a pan gravy. Remove everything from the pan except the drippins. Add flour to the drippins and cook on medium heat, scraping up the browned bits from the bottom of the pan, for 5 to 8 minutes, until toasty brown in color. Slowly add 1 cup chicken stock and stir until thickened, adding more stock if needed. Taste for salt and pepper—since the bird and the nest were both seasoned, the pan gravy might not need any more. Add 2 tablespoons butter and stir until it melts. Add ½ teaspoon fresh thyme leaves, if desired. Serve over rice. You can also freeze the gravy to use another time.

Enjoy. The bird is delicious on its own, but it's also perfect for using in other dishes the rest of the week, so make two at a time if you'd like to eat one now and use one later.

Who Said Gravy Has to Be Brown?

When I was talking with my Uncle Thomas about this book, one of the first things out of his mouth was, "Whatever you do, don't put Mama's gravy recipe in there!" I didn't remember Mama's gravy, but it turns out Uncle Thomas will never forget it. Apparently she was convinced that gravy needed to be brown. And being a child of the Depression and highly resourceful, she thought she'd figured out just the solution. She always kept a coffee percolator plugged in on the kitchen counter, so she would use the leftover coffee from the day before to color the gravy. It did, in fact, turn the gravy brown, but according to Uncle Thomas, it was inedible, an example of thrifty Southern ingenuity gone awry. Do not put coffee in your gravy—unless it's redeye gravy. My gravy is not brown. In fact, after seeing the expression on Uncle Thomas's face as he remembered the taste of his mother's brown gravy, I'm not sure I'll ever even be able to eat brown gravy again!

Note: If you'd like a delicious redeye gravy recipe, search for my friend Allan Benton's recipe. It really can't be improved upon. And please do use fresh, quality coffee. I have no idea how many days straight Mama would drink the same batch of coffee from her percolator, but I guarantee you any "extras" she used in her gravy would have been even older!

CHICKEN PILAU

One of my favorite things to do with an extra roasted chicken is to make this quintessential Lowcountry dish—spelled "pilau" but pronounced "purlow." It's another one of those surprising examples of Southern alchemy: The simplest and most inexpensive ingredients somehow transform into a unique dish with a super flavorful taste and texture. (I've included my recipe for sausage pilau as well, just because it's so good I couldn't leave it out!) Note that the rice on the bottom of the skillet will get a little crunchy. Not to fear. Just mix in this part and enjoy the crunch.

This recipe does make the skillet a little hard to clean. Once I've scraped it, I usually add about an inch of water and put it back on the stove on high heat. The simmering water pulls most of the bits off and makes it a cinch to clean. Then I dry it and rub in a dash of oil to keep the pot from getting rusty.

Makes 4 servings

2 cups shredded leftover roasted chicken

2 cups mixed cooked onions, carrots, and celery from the roasting pan, coarsely chopped with kitchen shears

4 cups cooked rice

1 cup water

Kosher salt and freshly ground black pepper

1 Combine the chicken, vegetables, rice, and water in a cast-iron skillet. Mix well. Cover and cook on medium heat about 10 minutes, or until heated through.

2 Taste and season with salt and pepper.

SAUSAGE PILAU

Makes 4 servings

1 pound bulk sausage or sausage
   links, casings removed
2 to 3 tablespoons bacon drippins
1 cup diced onion

1 cup chopped celery
2 cups cooked rice
¾ cup water, or more as needed
Kosher salt and freshly ground
   black pepper

Serving suggestion (optional): Hot
   sauce and chopped fresh flat-
   leaf parsley

1 Cook the sausage in a large skillet or saucepan, using the back of a spoon to break it into little pieces.
2 Leaving the grease in the skillet, remove the sausage to a paper bag to drain.

3 Add the bacon drippins to the skillet. Add the onion and celery and cook, stirring occasionally, for 8 to 10 minutes, until soft and the onion is golden.
4 Add the rice, cooked sausage, and water and mix well. Cover and cook on medium heat for 15 to 20 minutes, until heated through.
5 Taste and season with salt and pepper. Serve with hot sauce and chopped fresh parsley, if you wish.

Grits

You may wonder what grits are doing in a chapter about slow cooking, especially if you have been using instant or quick grits. The best grits are cooked slow slow slow. The longer they cook, the better they get. A slow cooker is one of the best ways to cook grits nice and slow without having to keep an eye on them. Callie's grits come from the Geechie Boy Mill on Edisto Island, South Carolina, where they coarse-grind their grits in an antique gristmill. No matter where you get your grits, be sure they are coarse-ground if you want the full, rich taste of grits rather than the soupy grayish gruel you might associate with diner grits. Coarse-ground grits come in white and yellow. I'm partial to white, but that's just a personal preference.

I make my grits with chicken stock rather than water to add extra flavor, or with milk instead of water to add creaminess. And I use more butter and salt than you would believe if I told you. So don't be stingy with those. Add a few generous grinds of the pepper mill as well. Grits really don't need much more adornment. That being said, I'm a sucker for cheese grits. Add the cheese during the last 5 minutes of cooking. My mother likes to add jalapeños. Experiment with your favorite flavorings.

Be sure to add liquid as needed so they don't dry out as they cook. When you are cooking grits, just accept that they are going to stick to the bottom of the pot. Leave this stuck-on layer alone and don't try to scrape it up while the grits cook. You can still stir as frequently as needed, but leave the stuck-on layer as is until after the pot has been emptied (at which point you may need to let that baby soak for a few days before you can peel the layer away).

Callie's
Charleston Biscuits
MADE BY HAND
CAROLINA
GRITS
CREAMIEST GRITS
in the CAROLINAS
NET WT. 1lb. (453g)

SLOW COOKER GRITS

This is a Christmas tradition for our family, but it's so delicious, you aren't going to want to limit yourself to one night a year. We put it on Christmas Eve right before setting out cookies for Santa. When we wake up, the grits are done. I serve them with chopped bacon, chopped green onions, and grated cheese. Since we have guests coming and going all day, this serves as a one-pot meal we can eat at our leisure without requiring any to-do.

Makes 10 to 12 servings

4 tablespoons (½ stick) butter
2 cups coarse-grind grits (not instant or quick-cooking!)
10 cups water or stock

Kosher salt and freshly ground black pepper
Optional: 1 cup milk, warmed

TOPPINGS
Chopped cooked bacon
Chopped green onions
Shredded sharp cheddar cheese

1 Use 2 tablespoons of the butter to coat the inside of the slow cooker, coming halfway up the sides.

2 Add the grits, the remaining butter, and the water or stock, and give it a good stir. Cover. Set on low for 8 to 10 hours.

3 When the grits are cooked, stir in salt and pepper to taste. Loosen with the milk if too thick.
4 If you wish, serve with one or more of the toppings.

PERFECTLY PESTO-ROASTED CHICKEN

This is one of my favorite variations on a roasted chicken. I came up with this recipe at the beginning of the school year—a time of transition for the whole family. We were switching from a summer of bare feet and variable bedtimes to the more rigid schooltime routine. Roasted chicken is a consistent source of comfort to me and my girls, especially when everything else is a little bit in flux. Even my summertime herbs had begun to die off that week in the cooler temperatures and I was determined to get one last taste of my mint and basil. So I combined them to make fresh pesto, and the whole family was delighted with the results, including a crust so crispy and delectable that my daughters thought it was fried!

If you have the time, dress the chicken with the pesto the day before or at least 2 hours prior to cooking. Let it come to room temperature before roasting.

Makes 4 to 6 servings

1½ lemons
1 whole chicken (3½ to 4 pounds), innards removed
1 teaspoon kosher salt
½ teaspoon freshly ground black pepper

3 carrots, cut in chunks
3 stalks celery, cut in chunks
2 large onions, cut in quarters

PESTO
⅓ cup pine nuts
1 cup loosely packed fresh basil
½ cup loosely packed fresh mint
½ cup grated Romano cheese
½ cup grated Parmesan cheese
½ cup olive oil

1 Squeeze the lemons over the chicken. Put the lemon shells inside the cavity. Season all over the chicken with the salt and pepper. Combine the carrots, celery, and onions in the center of a cast-iron skillet or shallow roasting pan to make a nest for the chicken.

2 Make the pesto: Toast the pine nuts in a small dry skillet on low heat until golden, 8 to 10 minutes. Let cool.

3 Combine the basil and mint in a mini food processor and pulse to chop a bit. Add the pine nuts, Romano, and Parmesan and pulse to mix. Slowly add the olive oil with the machine running, processing to a paste.

4 Rub the chicken all over with half of the pesto. (Refrigerate the leftover pesto, covered with a thin layer of olive oil, to toss with pasta or make bruschetta later.)

5 Place the chicken on the nest and put in the fridge, uncovered, for the day, or at least 2 hours.

6 About 3 hours before you want to serve, take the chicken out of the fridge to come to room temperature.

7 Preheat the oven to 375°F.

8 Place the chicken in the oven with the legs facing the rear. Rotate the pan back-to-front at the end of 30 minutes and again after another 30 minutes. Roast for a total of 1 hour 15 minutes to 1 hour 30 minutes, until the thigh temperature is 170°F and the juices run clear.

9 Remove the chicken from the oven, tent with foil, and let it rest 20 minutes before carving.

10 Carve and serve with the pan juices.

Roasted chicken and pimento cheese: two staples of my culinary and family life. They were bound to come together at some point! When we were fine-tuning the recipe for Callie's pimento cheese, we tasted batch after batch, adding a little of this and a little of that, trying to get it just right. This made for a refrigerator full of delicious pimento cheese. I had to come up with creative—and, of course, delicious—ways to use it. This recipe turned out to be one of the best.

There are two musts with this one. First, you must use bone-in chicken breasts. Skinless, boneless chicken breasts simply do not have the flavor of chicken on the bone. I never buy them. Second, the final step of putting the chicken under the broiler after the addition of the pimento cheese is essential. The broiler changes the whole texture of the meat—making it a little crispy on the outside while retaining the moisture inside. And it makes the pimento cheese get bubbly and ooze all over. So good.

Serve this with a simple roasted vegetable, such as asparagus.

Makes 4 servings

3 stalks celery, cut in half crosswise
1 large onion, chopped
8 to 10 small baby carrots
3 cloves garlic, cut in half
2 tablespoons olive oil

Kosher salt and freshly ground black pepper
4 skin-on, bone-in chicken breast halves
2 limes: 1 juiced, 1 cut in wedges
¼ cup pimento cheese (you know my favorite brand to use!)

¼ cup Southern Staple Salsa (page 87)
Crumbled tortilla chips
Serving suggestion: 1 avocado, pitted, peeled, and sliced

1 Preheat the oven to 275°F.
2 Toss all the bird's nest ingredients—celery, onion, carrots, and garlic—with 1 tablespoon of the olive oil, 1 teaspoon kosher salt, and ½ teaspoon pepper. Place in the bottom of a cast-iron skillet.
3 Toss the chicken breasts with the lime juice, 1 teaspoon kosher salt, and the remaining 1 tablespoon olive oil. Lay the breasts on the nest, skin side up. Cover with foil and roast for 1 hour 30 minutes, or until the juices run clear and the temperature reads 165°F.
4 Remove from the oven, uncover, and top each breast with a dollop of the pimento cheese.
5 Turn the oven to broil. Broil until the cheese softens and begins to bubble, 2 to 3 minutes.

6 Top with the chips and toast under the broiler; watch carefully, as they can burn quickly.
7 Top with the Southern Staple Salsa and serve with the lime wedges and avocado slices.

ROASTED PIMENTO CHEESE CHICKEN

Southern Staple Salsa

Makes 5 cups

⅓ cup minced sweet onion (Vidalia, Walla-Walla, or Texas 1015)
2 tablespoons vegetable oil
4 cups chopped tomatoes
½ cup diced roasted red bell pepper

½ cup diced orange bell pepper
½ cup diced green bell pepper
2 teaspoons minced garlic
3 green onions, chopped (white and green parts)
2 tablespoons olive oil

2 tablespoons rice vinegar or cider vinegar
1 teaspoon kosher salt
1 teaspoon Worcestershire sauce
1 teaspoon hot sauce, or more to taste

1 Cook the onion in the vegetable oil until translucent. Remove to a large bowl and let cool.
2 Add the tomatoes, bell peppers, garlic, and green onions. Stir in the olive oil, vinegar, and salt. Taste and adjust the salt. Stir in the Worcestershire and hot sauce. Allow the flavors to marry at least 1 hour before using. You can use leftovers as a dip or condiment.

MIDWEEK MAPLE-GLAZED PORK LOIN

When I was on my own for the first time and in my first apartment, pork tenderloin was a safe staple I made many times over. It was easy to find at the grocery store, the directions were right on the plastic bag it came in (already marinated, no less!), and it required little more effort than putting it in the oven. Well, I ate my lifetime limit of pork tenderloin during that first year. Years later, somewhere along the way, I stumbled on pork loin. Where a tenderloin is lean, a pork loin has more fat and so more flavor. Where a tenderloin is relatively skinny and prone to dry out during cooking, a loin is meatier and holds moisture and flavor much better. This particular recipe was inspired by a glorious food-, fun-, and pork-filled Southern Foodways Alliance Taste of the South gathering at Blackberry Farm in Walland, Tennessee. I'm not usually a big breakfast person, but the breakfasts at Blackberry Farm were irresistible. That weekend I ate what should be illegal amounts of their maple-pepper bacon, and by the time I got home I was already craving more of that blend of sugary sweet maple with salty savory pork and wanted to take it from breakfast to a dinner entree. This recipe was a success at our family table, and everyone helped themselves to seconds. It has become a star staple in our house, sure to stick around longer than my unfortunate pork-in-a-bag habit.

Makes 4 to 6 servings

1 boneless pork loin (about 4 pounds)
Kosher salt and freshly ground black pepper
1 tablespoon olive oil

3 carrots, cut lengthwise in quarters
1 large yellow onion, cut in quarters
8 small potatoes, cut in half
½ cup maple syrup

¼ cup Dijon mustard
1 tablespoon white wine vinegar
3 cloves garlic, minced
1 teaspoon chopped fresh rosemary

1 Preheat the oven to 375°F.
2 Season the pork, using about ¼ teaspoon salt per side and plenty of pepper.
3 Heat the oil in a cast-iron skillet on medium-high heat. Sear the pork on all sides, cooking about 3 minutes per side. Remove from the pan and set aside.

4 Place the carrots, onion, and potatoes in the bottom of the pan. Place the pork on top of the vegetables. Combine the maple syrup, mustard, vinegar, garlic, and rosemary, and drizzle over the pork and vegetables.
5 Cover with foil and roast 1 hour 15 minutes, or until a digital thermometer registers 135°F.

6 Remove the pork to a cutting board to rest for 15 minutes. Turn the oven to broil, and broil 3 to 6 minutes to crisp the potatoes and vegetables.
7 Slice the pork and serve with the vegetables and pan juices.

SLOW COOKER PULLED PORK WITH VINEGAR-BASED BBQ SAUCE

My Uncle Larry and Aunt Martha live in Summerville, South Carolina, where the annual Flowertown Festival is pretty much the biggest event of the year. Uncle Larry and Aunt Martha always host a party for family and friends during the festival, and Uncle Larry's BBQ is the featured event. He gets up at the crack of dawn to put on the Boston butts so the BBQ is cooked nice and slow and is just right by the time the guests arrive. His BBQ is so good, I gave him the nickname "The King of Butts," and I think he likes it!

He and Aunt Martha live in an old house with a huge porch and sprawling front and backyards.

Everyone from that side of the family comes and brings a covered dish—macaroni and cheese, casseroles, every kind of cookie and Bundt cake you can imagine—and everyone brings his or her own lawn chair to sit in. Children are running and playing. People are coming and going. This party just keeps going until all the food runs out.

One of my favorite things about this annual family get-together is that Mama's surviving sisters are always there. Mama was one of nine children, and her sisters Sara, Eddie, Lois, and Norma still make it to the party every year. And they look just like her! They are petite, precious

---

1 (6- to 8-pound) bone-in Boston butt or pork shoulder roast
1 teaspoon kosher salt
1½ teaspoons freshly ground black pepper

2 cups white vinegar
1½ cups packed light brown sugar
1 cup fresh lemon juice

1 tablespoon chili powder
1½ teaspoons smoked paprika
½ teaspoon ground cumin, or more to taste

---

1 Season the pork with the salt and 1 teaspoon of the pepper. Place fat side down in a slow cooker. Combine the vinegar, brown sugar, lemon juice, chili powder, paprika, cumin, and the remaining ½ teaspoon pepper. Mix well to dissolve the sugar and pour half over the pork roast. Reserve the rest for serving.
2 Cover and cook on low about 10 hours. Turn the pork a few times during cooking. After about 9 hours, insert a thermometer in the meat. It is done at 195°F. You will see that the meat has pulled from the bone and shreds easily.
3 Remove the pork to a platter and turn off the cooker. Strain the juices into a pot and skim off the fat.
4 Put the pork back in the cooker. Remove and discard the bone and any dark, stringy bits and fatty pieces. Use two forks and "pull" the meat into shreds.
5 Heat the strained juices with the reserved marinade, pour over the meat, mix well, and serve.

Note: I like to serve my Brown Sugar–Bourbon BBQ Sauce (page 225) and Southern Staple Salsa (page 87) with this.

women, not one of them five feet tall. When I see them, I think of Mama and miss her dearly, and I am so thankful that my children get to spend time with them and get to run wild all over Uncle Larry and Aunt Martha's yard just like my cousins and I did when we were their age. This recipe is inspired by the King of Butts and all he does to keep our family gathering together and celebrating each other.

Makes 6 to 8 servings

Even though my brothers, Kinnon and Miles, are in their twenties now, I still think of them as growing boys. They love coming over for hearty, rib-sticking food, and this beef stew, especially served over grits with a side of French bread, does the trick without being too thick like some beef stews. Make this ahead of time if you can—it gets better the longer it sits. And one recipe makes a large amount for those growing-boy appetites. Sometimes I even let them take home leftovers.

The turnips in the recipe are a nod to Mama, who used them in her recipe, probably because they were inexpensive and she could buy them at one of the roadside stands close to her house. But they are more than just nostalgia. I love to wash the leaves and add them at the end. The leaves give beautiful color, vitamins, and taste to this one-dish meal. My affinity for turnips aside, potatoes or any other root vegetable can certainly be substituted. But if you haven't ever cooked with turnips, this is a great way to introduce them into your cuisine.

You can also use the sour cream as a dip for veggie crudités.

Makes 6 servings

HERBED SOUR CREAM

1 cup sour cream
1 clove garlic, minced
1 tablespoon minced fresh mint
1 tablespoon minced fresh flat-leaf parsley
1 tablespoon minced fresh basil
1 tablespoon thinly sliced green onion (1 very thin, small onion, white and green parts)
Kosher salt and freshly ground black pepper

LIGHTER BEEF STEW

4 slices thick-cut bacon, diced
2 pounds beef stew meat
1½ teaspoons kosher salt
½ teaspoon freshly ground black pepper
⅔ cup all-purpose flour
1 tablespoon butter
2 cups peeled pearl onions
4 cloves garlic
2 or 3 sprigs fresh thyme
1½ cups hearty red wine (such as cabernet sauvignon)
3 cups canned beef consommé
2½ cups sliced carrots, cut on the diagonal
20 small turnips, peeled, stems and leaves reserved
Serving suggestion: Grits or steamed rice

1 Make the herbed sour cream: Mix together all the ingredients, seasoning to taste with salt and pepper. Refrigerate at least 1 hour to let the flavors marry.
2 Make the beef stew: Fry the bacon in a stockpot or Dutch oven until crisp. Remove the bacon to a paper bag to drain. Leave the drippins in the pot.
3 Season the stew meat with the salt and pepper. Put the flour in a resealable plastic bag and add the meat. Seal the bag and shake to coat the meat.
4 Working in batches if necessary, brown the meat in the drippins. Remove the meat to a platter.
5 Melt the butter into the drippins. Add the onions and cook until golden brown, 8 to 10 minutes. Reserve the onions with the meat.
6 Add the garlic, thyme, and wine to the drippins. Scrape up any browned bits. Cover and simmer 20 minutes.
7 Add the bacon, onions, stew meat, and beef consommé. Bring to a boil, then reduce the heat and simmer 2 hours.
8 Add the carrots and turnips and simmer 30 to 40 minutes, until the meat and vegetables are tender. In the final 10 minutes, add the turnip stems and leaves.
9 Serve over grits or rice, topped with the herbed sour cream.

BEEF-MUSHROOM-BARLEY SOUP

This is a wintertime staple at our house. I often double the recipe and share with someone who's feeling under the weather or otherwise in need of some comfort food—accompanied by biscuits, of course. Or I freeze the leftovers for another night. If I have a busy week ahead, I refrigerate it and reheat as much as I need for suppers and lunch until it's all gone.

My father and stepmother, Caroline, gave me a large yellow Le Creuset Dutch oven one Christmas—it's cast iron under that enamel! I love seeing the big yellow pot on my stove and knowing it's full of some soul-warming soup at the ready. It just makes me happy on a gray day.

I like to serve this over rice. For a side I take sliced country bread, put Brie and a sprinkling of chopped green onions on top, and put it under the broiler for a minute. A wonderfully hearty meal.

Makes 6 to 8 servings

4 slices thick-cut bacon, cut in large cubes
2 cups diced onions
1½ cups sliced mushrooms
3 pounds beef sirloin, cut in bite-size cubes
Kosher salt and freshly ground black pepper

¼ cup all-purpose flour
Optional: Vegetable oil
2 tablespoons hearty red wine
4 cups fresh or frozen vegetables of your choice: corn kernels, cut green beans, butter beans, chopped tomatoes, chopped carrots

6 cups canned beef consommé
2 cups water
1 bay leaf
3 sprigs fresh thyme
4 sprigs fresh flat-leaf parsley
¾ cup pearled barley

1 Fry the bacon in a stockpot or Dutch oven until crisp. Remove the bacon to a paper bag to drain. Leave the drippins in the pot.

2 Add the onions and mushrooms to the drippins and cook until the onions are translucent and the mushrooms are shiny, 6 to 8 minutes.

3 While the onions and mushrooms are cooking, season the beef with ½ teaspoon salt and ¼ teaspoon pepper. Working in batches if necessary, place in a resealable plastic bag with the flour, seal, and shake until the meat is well coated.

4 Remove the onions and mushrooms to a plate. Add a little vegetable oil to the drippins if the pot looks dry. Brown the meat on all sides; you may need to do this in batches. Do not crowd the pot. Reserve the meat with the onions and mushrooms.

5 Pour in the wine and scrape up all the flavorful browned bits with a wooden spoon. Return the bacon, meat, and onions and mushrooms to the pot. Stir in the vegetables, consommé, and water. Bring to a boil, then reduce the heat to a simmer.

6 Tie the bay leaf, thyme, and parsley into a bundle with kitchen twine. Add to the soup with the barley. Simmer 2 hours, or until the beef is tender. Remove herb bundle. Taste and adjust the salt and pepper.

Note: With soups like this, there is usually that layer stuck to the pot that if you try to scrape up while cooking will become brown burnt pieces floating in your soup. Resist the urge to scrape once everything is in the pot.

MILEY'S PORK AND VEGETABLE SOUP

My wonderful friend Miley and I both started college together at Carolina (that's University of SOUTH Carolina, of course) and became immediate fast friends. The first weekend I went home from school, my father was asking me about new friends I'd made, and when I told him about Miley, he said, "You mean L.B.'s daughter?" The South is a small world, and it turned out my father had grown up with Miley's mother. Knowing that our parents had grown up together solidified our relationship and gave us a sense that our friendship was meant to be. Miley and I have been close ever since, and we both have three girls almost exactly the same age. The only "problem" with Miley is that she is so darn healthy! This delicious soup is inspired by one of her recipes that I've always loved. I've added my requisite bacon drippins to it just to get under her skin.

Makes 6 to 8 servings

2 tablespoons bacon drippins or vegetable oil
1 pound ground pork or turkey
1 teaspoon ground cumin
¼ teaspoon chili powder
¼ teaspoon dried oregano
½ teaspoon kosher salt
¼ teaspoon freshly ground black pepper
1 large onion, finely chopped
3 stalks celery, chopped
1 large carrot, finely chopped

2 cloves garlic, minced
1 (4-ounce) can chopped roasted green chiles
1 cup water
2 cups chicken stock
1 (16-ounce) package frozen corn kernels or 3 cups fresh (cut from about 5 ears)
1 (15-ounce) can black beans, drained and rinsed
1½ cups Southern Staple Salsa (page 87)

TORTILLA STRIPS
6 flour tortillas
Olive or vegetable oil

TOPPINGS
¼ cup chopped fresh cilantro
1 avocado, pitted, peeled, and sliced
Sour cream
Shredded cheddar cheese

1 Heat 1 tablespoon of the bacon drippins in a stockpot. Add the meat and brown, using the back of a spoon to break it into little pieces. Stir in the cumin, chili powder, oregano, salt, and pepper.
2 Once browned, scoop out the meat and set it aside. Add the remaining 1 tablespoon drippins to the pot. Add the onion, celery, and carrot and cook until the onion is translucent. Stir in the garlic and chiles and cook 5 minutes. Add the water and stock and scrape up all the bits from the bottom of the pot. Return the meat to the pot and add the corn, black beans, and Southern Staple Salsa. Bring to a boil, then reduce the heat and simmer at least 1 hour.
3 Make the tortilla strips: Preheat the oven to 350°F. Brush the tortillas with oil. Place one on top of another in a stack. Use shears or a sharp knife to cut in ¼-inch-wide strips. Spread the strips on a baking sheet and bake for 8 to 10 minutes, until lightly browned.

4 Serve the soup with the tortilla strips and toppings.

Variation: The soup may be prepared in a slow cooker. Cook the meat with the spices, onion, celery, carrot, garlic, and chiles in a skillet. Remove them to the slow cooker. Pour the water into the skillet and scrape to loosen the bits. Add that to the meat and vegetables in the slow cooker along with the stock, corn, beans, and salsa. Cover and cook on low for 5 to 8 hours.

WHITE BEAN AND COLLARD SOUP

This recipe will forever have a happy association in my mind. Callie's Charleston Biscuits was going to be on the show *Unwrapped* on the Food Network, so I decided to have a viewing party at my house for the Callie's bakers, family, and friends. How to feed about twenty people and make sure I didn't miss the show myself? A soup party. I remember not only the shared excitement of seeing the Callie's staff on TV, but also the convivial feeling of the party as everyone at their leisure fixed bowls of soup, added whatever toppings they liked, picked up a spoon and cloth napkin, and walked from room to room with bowl in hand, sitting a moment here to talk to one person, then moving to another room and talking to someone else, and then gathering around the TV for the big viewing. It was casual, intimate, and a day of excitement and fellowship.

A soup party is a delightful plan for any occasion when you'd rather not set the table or adhere to any kind of schedule. You can prepare the soup ahead of time, let it simmer all day and through-out the party, let people serve themselves—and then the after-party cleanup is little more than putting bowls and spoons in the dishwasher and putting soapy water in the soup pot to soak. The secret to making the soup part of the entertain-ment itself is to take the time to prepare plenty of toppings your guests can mix and match and add to their soup. Don't skip this step. And make enough to allow for seconds . . .

Makes 6 servings

½ pound pancetta, sliced ¼ inch thick and then cut into small dice
½ white onion, coarsely chopped
2 carrots, coarsely chopped
2 stalks celery, coarsely chopped
1 tablespoon butter
2 (15-ounce) cans white beans, drained and rinsed
4 cups chicken stock
2 cups water

4 cloves garlic, chopped
½ cup whipping cream
1 bunch fresh collards, stems re-moved, washed and chopped
Kosher salt and freshly ground black pepper

TOPPINGS
4 tomatoes
Olive oil

Leaves from 1 bunch fresh basil
Kosher salt and freshly ground black pepper
1 (8- to 10-count) can artichoke hearts, drained
Parmesan cheese, in 1 piece
French baguette
Garlic cloves, cut in half

1 Cook the pancetta in a stock-pot until browned and crispy. Remove to a paper bag to drain and reserve for the toppings.
2 Place the onion, carrots, and celery in a food processer and pulse until almost paste-like.
3 Melt the butter into the drip-pins in the stockpot. Add the vegetable "paste" and cook 20 minutes, stirring occasionally so the vegetables don't burn.
4 Stir in the beans, stock, water, and chopped garlic. Mix well. Bring to a boil, then reduce the heat and simmer 1 hour.
5 Use an immersion blender to puree the soup, or mash with a potato masher in the pot, or strain and puree the beans in a blender with a little of the liquid. (Caution: Use a towel to cover the lid of the blender and only fill to one-half capacity when pu-reeing hot liquids. Be very care-ful.) If using a blender, return the puree and liquid to the pot.
6 Add the cream and collards and simmer 30 to 45 minutes.
7 Make the toppings: Put the reserved pancetta in a serving bowl. Chop the tomatoes and put in another bowl. Mix in 1 teaspoon olive oil and 4 of the basil leaves (torn), and season with salt and pepper. Put the remaining whole basil leaves in another bowl.
8 Heat a grill pan. Toss the artichoke hearts with 1 teaspoon olive oil and grill 2 to 3 minutes per side or until grill marks form. Chop and put in another bowl.
9 Use a vegetable peeler to shave thin strips of Parmesan.
10 Slice the bread ½ inch thick, brush with olive oil, and grill 30 to 45 seconds to toast. Rub with the cut garlic cloves.

Note: To reheat the soup, add more stock or water, as it thickens when cooled.

SPLIT PEA SOUP WITH SHAVED COUNTRY HAM AND BUTTERMILK BISCUIT CROUTONS

I fell in love with split pea soup in New York City. I couldn't get enough. I ate it three or four times a week from the same soup shop on the corner near my office. Even on hot New York summer days . . . split pea soup. It tastes so creamy without any cream. My tastes have grown more sophisticated in some ways, but the simplicity of this soup never gets old to me. Add the shaved country ham and buttermilk biscuit croutons, and I couldn't be happier in one of New York's finest restaurants.

This recipe includes a base of carrots, celery, and onions used in so many good soups, including my white bean and collard soup. The use of an aromatic vegetable base is nearly universal, with regional variations and additions, referred to as "the trinity," "soffrito," "mirepoix," and other terms in other languages. The vegetable base gives soups a depth and complexity of flavor that goes far beyond the more obvious ingredients—it takes a simple soup to the next level of craveworthy taste, where you feel you have to make that particular soup that very day and you have to have another bowl after you finish the first.

Makes 6 to 8 servings

5 tablespoons butter
1 tablespoon olive oil
1 cup diced carrots
1 cup diced onion
1 cup diced celery
2 cloves garlic, minced

½ pound paper-thin shaved country ham, cut in thin strips
¾ teaspoon smoked paprika
1 bay leaf
6 to 8 cups water
2 cups split green peas

Kosher salt and freshly ground black pepper
Whole nutmeg
Buttermilk Biscuit Croutons (page 32)
Grandmama's Relish (page 100)

1 Melt 1 tablespoon of the butter into the oil in a stockpot. Add the carrots, onion, celery, and garlic and cook on medium heat, stirring occasionally, until the onion is translucent. Stir in the ham and cook until the ham gets crispy. Add the paprika, bay leaf, 6 cups water, and the peas. Bring to a boil, stir well, reduce the heat, and simmer 2 hours. Add up to 2 cups water if the soup thickens too much.
2 Taste and season with salt and pepper.
3 Just before serving, remove the bay leaf and stir in 8 scrapes fresh nutmeg and the remaining 4 tablespoons butter.
4 Top each serving with croutons and relish.

Note: For a creamier soup, use an immersion blender or puree three-quarters of the soup in a blender. (Caution: Use a towel to cover the lid of the blender and only fill to one-half capacity when pureeing hot liquids. Be very careful.)

GRANDMAMA'S RELISH

Makes 4 cups

1 (2-pound) head cabbage, cored
2 cups sugar
2 cups cider vinegar
1 tablespoon kosher salt

1 tablespoon mustard seeds
1 tablespoon ground turmeric
2 teaspoons celery seeds
1 onion, finely minced
1 red bell pepper, seeded and finely minced

3 to 5 jalapeño chiles, seeded and finely minced (adjust to your preference; 3 give this relish a "kick")

1 Grate the cabbage very fine in a food processor. Drain in a colander.

2 Combine the sugar, vinegar, salt, mustard seeds, turmeric, and celery seeds in a nonreactive saucepan. Boil 5 minutes to dissolve the sugar.

3 Combine the cabbage, onion, bell pepper, and jalapeños in a large plastic or glass container. Mix well. Pour the vinegar mixture over the vegetables and mix. Cover and refrigerate. This will keep for up to 5 days in the fridge.

BLACK-EYED PEAS OVER RICE

Makes 6 cups cooked beans

1 pound dried black-eyed peas
4 slices thick-cut bacon, chopped
2 cups chicken stock

About 3 cups water
1 teaspoon kosher salt

½ teaspoon freshly ground black
pepper

1 Rinse the peas and pick through for stones. Place in a deep container and add enough water to cover by 2 inches. Soak overnight. Drain and rinse the soaked peas.
2 Fry the bacon in a stockpot or Dutch oven until cooked but not crisp, 3 to 5 minutes.

3 Add the peas, stock, and 2 cups water. Bring to a simmer, skim any foam that forms, cover, and cook 45 minutes.
4 Taste to see if the peas have softened. If so, add the salt and pepper; if not, cook 15 minutes more and taste again. When softened, add the salt and pepper.

5 Adjust the cooking liquid with water if it gets too thick. Make sure a thin layer of liquid covers the peas. Simmer 60 to 90 minutes, until very tender.
6 Serve over rice or use to make Spicy Black-Eyed Pea Salad (page 102).

BUTTER BEANS

When I was young, a lot of nights it was just me and my dad. Complicated or multidish dinners were not part of our routine. Yet my taste buds did not suffer one bit. One of our frequent meals was butter beans on rice. No meat served with it, and no adornment added other than a pat of butter. Eat it on a plate. Eat it in a bowl. Heat it back up the next day and eat it again. I loved it then, and I love it now.

I buy enough fresh butter beans—also known as lima beans—in the summer to last all year.

I separate them into resealable plastic bags, each with about 3 cups of beans, and put them in the freezer so I can pull them out as needed throughout the year. Mama always had a pot of butter beans on the stovetop right next to her steamer of rice—they really do work well with almost any meal or, as my father and I can attest, as a meal themselves.

Makes 3 cups

1 slice thick-cut bacon, chopped
3 cups chicken stock

3 cups water
3 cups fresh butter beans, shelled

Kosher salt and freshly ground
black pepper

1 Fry the bacon in a saucepan large enough to hold the beans and liquid. Cook until the fat renders but the bacon is not crispy. Add the stock and water and bring to a boil. Add the but-

ter beans and reduce the heat to a simmer. Cover and cook 30 to 45 minutes, until tender.
2 Taste the beans for tenderness around 25 minutes. If tender, add salt and pepper.

3 When the beans are fully cooked, turn off the heat and let the pot rest on the stove up to 1 hour. Serve as is or over rice.

SPICY BLACK-EYED PEA SALAD

Makes 6 cups

6 cups drained cooked black-eyed peas (see page 101)

4 green onions, thinly sliced into rings (white and green parts)

2 red bell peppers, seeded and diced

1 green bell pepper, seeded and diced

¼ cup olive oil

2 tablespoons cider vinegar

2 teaspoons sriracha (Asian chili sauce) or your favorite hot sauce

Kosher salt and freshly ground black pepper

1 Combine the peas, green onions, and bell peppers in a large bowl. Stir in the oil, vinegar, and hot sauce. Taste and season with salt and pepper. Cover and refrigerate overnight for the flavors to marry.

2 Taste after chilling and adjust the salt and pepper. Serve chilled or at room temperature.

Dried peas and beans have to be among the most nutritious, inexpensive, filling, and tasty options in the grocery store—all of which make them a favorite for Southerners. Lowcountry people in particular have long enjoyed black-eyed peas, cow peas, or field peas on New Years Day on their own or in hopping john (peas cooked with onion, bacon, and rice in a rice steamer) for good luck in the new year along with collards to ensure the new year brings more money than the year previous. This recipe is wonderful any time of the year, either served over rice as a meal in itself or cooled down and put into a salad for a summertime side or salsa-like dip.

I like my black-eyed peas nice and soft, which means cooking them slow. I love checking on them and seeing them change throughout the day as the broth goes from translucent to cloudy to an almost creamy consistency. You'll notice how few ingredients this recipe requires and then be amazed by how such simple beginnings transform hour by hour into a Southern classic you really can't improve upon.

SALADS AND SANDWICHES

This chapter is less about technique and more about easy no-cooking-required salads and sandwiches that we in the South like to "put together," especially during the warmer months when no one wants to stand in front of a hot stove. Summertime in the South is famously hot and humid. But we really don't mind the heat *all* that much. We will complain about it, but that is simply a requisite part of the conversation as we sit on the porch, dock, beach, or boat. And that is a lot of what we do in the summer: We find a sliver of shade or a bit of water and sit there talking and telling stories and, of course, eating and drinking something cool in the process.

Growing up, one of the places where my family retreated from the heat for a few weeks every summer was Grandmama's lake house on Lake Lure in the mountains of North Carolina. Several of the recipes in this chapter are Grandmama's—all foods I associate with summer and time spent with family. At the lake we would start the morning with a breakfast of cheese toast under the broiler with a local tomato slice and discussion of the most exciting topic of the day: what we would eat for lunch and supper. Plans made, we would then spend the rest of the daylight hours jumping off the boathouse, waterskiing, and riding around in the pontoon boat.

The lake house itself wasn't fancy, but the time we spent there was simply happy. Grandmama and my grandfather, Papa, were so in love. Papa sang Tony Bennett songs to her and was always the life of the party. He was a jeweler by trade, and he repaired anything that needed to be fixed around the house and dock and built benches and other additions as well. His jeweler's magnifying glasses sat on top of his head at all times so he

could pull them down as needed to see whatever he was doing. He was also a health nut of sorts and a vegetarian before anyone in their circle had ever heard of being vegetarian. But Grandmama would fix his plate with whatever goodness she had made anyway. "Now, Billy won't eat that," she'd say, but she'd still spoon it onto his plate. It was all part of a beautiful routine. Late afternoon on the lake meant cocktail hour, with people coming over on their pontoon boats for a drink or us taking our pontoon for a long boat ride with daiquiris for the adults and always tomato sandwiches and pigs in a blanket as an onboard hors d'oeuvre.

Now my mother, Callie, is the matriarch of the lake. She plans much more elaborate menus even weeks in advance of our trip, taking the lake meals to a whole new level and even bringing a cooler of meat with her from home. We take long walks each morning, which inevitably include a debate on what we'll fix that day. She'll usually make a turkey breast right off the bat so we'll have fresh turkey for sandwiches we can eat on the dock or the boat. And, of course, we make all variety of side dishes based on the delicious local produce we pick up from the stands that line the curvy mountain roads around the lake.

All of us spend our days in bathing suits and cover-ups like we did when I was little, and we all still jockey for the spot closest to the fan on the screened porch. Just like I did as a child, my girls jump off the boathouse into the cold lake water, help pick out peaches from the produce stands, enjoy early evening cruises on the pontoon boat as they eavesdrop on the grown-up conversations, and feast on *their* grandmother's good cooking.

For me food is an essential part of almost all of my memories. Making the same recipes my grandmother made and standing next to my mother in the kitchen at the lake as she carries on—and adds to—our family's culinary tradition, I hope I'm making food memories for my girls that they will want to re-create one day standing side by side in the lake house kitchen or wherever their summers may take them. I hope that your food takes you places—and if you have a recipe, even one as simple as my mother's perfect tomato sandwich, that transports you to a happy place or time, write it down. Your grandchildren will thank you later as they get to experience your food memory for themselves and eventually make it their own.

MOM'S PERFECT
TOMATO SANDWICHES

This recipe is the centerpiece of all of our summertime family activities and the essence of everything I love about summer: simplicity, freshness, local flavor, drip-down-your-arm juiciness, and hands young and old reaching in to pick one up as the family gathers together for the summer. The main thing about this sandwich is the quality of the tomato. The tomato must be fresh and ripe or else the sandwich will not change your life the way it's meant to.

Makes 1 sandwich

Ripe tomatoes
Pepperidge Farms white sandwich-style bread, crusts removed
Hellmann's mayonnaise
Kosher salt and freshly ground black pepper

Peel (see page 157) and slice tomatoes. Slices should be ¼-inch thick. Slather 2 slices of bread with generous amounts of mayonnaise and place 3 to 4 tomato slices on each slice. Generously salt and pepper the tomatoes and assemble. Cut in quarters and serve immediately.

CARRIE'S TIPS

Avocados Avocados are the perfect summer ingredient. Even though they aren't Southern in themselves, they go so well with Southern foods and give a cool, creamy oomph to everything. To extract the "meat," cut around the avocado the long way, separate the halves, whack the pit with the knife blade, turn it slightly to loosen, pull out the pit, and discard. I run my knife around the entire edge. I cut the meat on the diagonal for slices, and then on the other diagonal to dice. Then I squeeze out the pieces.

Bread Crusts To serve sandwiches as finger sandwiches or an hors d'oeuvre, I usually remove the crusts. When I want to get this done ahead of time, I slice the crusts off stacks of about four slices at a time and put the decrusted slices back in the bag until I'm ready to make the sandwiches. I save the crusts for later, when I put them in the food processor to make breadcrumbs. (For more on making breadcrumbs, see page 196, step 6.) When serving the sandwiches on a tray, I like to press finely chopped herbs onto the sides of the sandwiches for a fancy presentation.

Mayonnaise The great Southern debate: Hellmann's or Duke's mayonnaise? My father insists on Duke's, but he is in the minority in our family. Only Hellmann's crosses these lips!

DILLICIOUS CUCUMBER SANDWICHES

I love cucumber sandwiches. I love the crunch of the cucumbers and the creaminess of the spread. I love them chilled before serving so they're super cold. I even love the way they look on a tray. The spread for these sandwiches on its own is superb as a dip for crudités or almost anything. One night I made cucumber sandwiches to take to a cocktail party. When I got home, I wanted a snack. What I really wanted was a cucumber sandwich, but I was out of cucumbers and bread. I did have some of the spread left, but the only other thing I could find in the house to eat it on was potato chips. So I dipped the chips in the spread—and could not stop eating. Thank goodness we only had one bag of chips.

Makes 3 cups spread

1 cup mayonnaise
2 (8-ounce) blocks cream cheese,
    at room temperature
½ cup finely minced onion
½ cup finely minced dill
¼ cup finely minced fresh mint

2 cloves garlic, minced
¼ teaspoon kosher salt
⅛ teaspoon freshly ground black
    pepper
White sandwich-style bread,
    crusts removed

Peeled cucumber slices, drained,
    4 to 6 slices per sandwich
    (I prefer the seedless English
    variety, but any variety is fine)

1 Combine the mayonnaise, cream cheese, onion, dill, mint, garlic, salt, and pepper. Beat well or whip with a handheld mixer or in a stand mixer.

2 Spread 1 to 2 tablespoons between 2 slices of bread. Place cucumbers on one slice of the bread and top with the remaining slice of bread. Cut in quarters.

Finger Sandwiches

There is something about finger sandwiches and Southern weddings. You would think there is nothing particularly elegant about tiny sandwiches cut up into triangles with the crusts removed. And maybe there isn't anything elegant about it—maybe it's just that they are so darned good! Traditional Southern weddings are not typically sit-down dinners. That is a rather recent practice. They used to be held later at night to take advantage of the cooler temperatures, and so the food usually consisted of hors d'oeuvres and cocktails rather than five-course plated meals. Maybe the tradition of finger sandwiches started from that. I don't know, but when I got married, I had Mom's tomato sandwiches at the reception and other finger sandwiches on our bus from the church to the reception.

Yes, a bus! John and I got married in downtown Charleston, but I wanted the reception to be in Rockville where I had spent so many wonderful days on the water with family. So we arranged for a bus to take the wedding party from downtown to Rockville, thirty minutes away. On the bus we had finger sandwiches made by the legendary Mrs. Hamby. Fran Hamby and her catering company make all sorts of fabulous things, but she is most famous for her finger sandwiches. People walk into parties, notice right off the bat by sight if the finger sandwiches are Hamby's or not, and if so, grab a handful before they are all gone.

That night, the wedding party on the bus enjoyed the classic trifecta: chicken salad, egg salad, and shrimp salad. Then we had such a good time at the reception that John and I really didn't want to leave! My cousin Jimmy took us away by boat as planned, but we had hatched a plan with the bus driver.

Jimmy drove us back to a spot alongside the busy highway between Rockville and Charleston, me still in my wedding gown and John in his tux. We got out and stuck our thumbs out in dramatic fashion as the bus taking the wedding party back to Charleston came along. The driver pulled over and we got on, to the surprise of our friends. Then we all rode into Charleston munching on boiled peanuts (party favors from the wedding) along the way before disembarking downtown to continue the celebration.

Elegance has its place, but Southern celebrations are all about the more authentic guts of the thing. The taste is more important than the presentation, and fun always trumps "the way it's supposed to be done."

BBQ CHICKEN SALAD
BISCUITS

I develop many of my favorite recipes from happy accidents. At Callie's Biscuit House we often have what we like to call "staff meals." Charleston summers are hot, humid, and downright oppressive at times, and the preferred escapes—beaching, boating, and napping in a cold dark room—do not include baking biscuits. So one steamy morning I wanted to make an off-the-cuff staff meal to give the bakers a little relief and appreciation.

I had leftovers from a very moist and delicious BBQ chicken, so I decided to make chicken salad for sandwiches. When I got to the bakery, I realized I had forgotten the loaf of bread. So instead of sliced bread, we ate the chicken salad on hot buttermilk biscuits right out of the oven. I'd never have put it together that way if we hadn't had to think on our feet, but the cold salad with the hot pillowy biscuits and a dab of cold BBQ sauce was a sweet, tangy, savory combination of flavors and textures I have since repeated countless times. Add a slice of Grandmama's Fresh Pickles (page 111), and it's divine.

If you don't want to cook the chicken fresh, you can use 6 cups leftover roasted or rotisserie chicken instead.

Makes 12 servings

CHICKEN
12 skin-on, bone-in chicken thighs
1 teaspoon kosher salt
½ teaspoon freshly ground black pepper
½ teaspoon smoked paprika
¼ teaspoon dried thyme

SAUCE
¾ to 1 cup mayonnaise
2 stalks celery, finely diced
1 tablespoon minced onion
1 tablespoon whipping cream or milk
Kosher salt and freshly ground black pepper

12 biscuits, warm from the oven
BBQ sauce (your favorite, or Brown Sugar–Bourbon BBQ Sauce, page 225)
Optional: Grandmama's Fresh Pickles (page 111)

1 Make the chicken: Preheat the oven to 375°F. Place the chicken thighs in a cast-iron skillet, skin side down. Mix the salt, pepper, paprika, and thyme and sprinkle over the thighs. Bake 30 to 40 minutes, until a digital thermometer inserted into the thigh registers 170°F.
2 Let the chicken cool. Remove the skin and bones and chop the meat into cubes.
3 Make the sauce: Combine the mayonnaise, celery, onion, and cream. Mix well and add the cooled chicken. Taste and season with salt and pepper.
4 Serve on the biscuits with a smattering of BBQ sauce. Add a slice of pickle, if you like.

GRANDMAMA'S FRESH PICKLES

These "quick" pickles were always in Grandmama's refrigerator, and now Mom and I both make them. Since they're fresh and meant to be eaten within a few days, they require none of the traditional pickling or putting-up processes like sterilizing and sealing jars. In fact, I make these in a gallon-size resealable plastic bag that I stick in my fridge. I use a slotted spoon to remove however much I need at a time. What I love about these cukes and onions is that you can eat them as a condiment, putting slices on burgers, sandwiches, or BBQ, or you can treat them like a salad and serve a whole spoonful as a side for any dish. These crispy cukes and sweet onions complement ribs, anything with BBQ sauce, fried chicken, and fish, and they go well with Asian dishes, too. They also taste good when you're looking in the fridge for something else and decide to stick a spoon in the bag for a sneaky little snack.

Makes about 1 quart

2 pounds cucumbers, sliced to yield 6 cups (I prefer the seedless English variety, but any variety is fine)

4 cups thinly sliced Vidalia onions (about 2 large onions)
2 teaspoons sugar
2 teaspoons kosher salt

4 cups cold water
⅓ cup cider vinegar
2 to 3 whole sprigs fresh dill

1 Combine the cucumbers and onions in a large bowl. Dissolve the sugar and salt in the water. Add the vinegar and fresh dill. Pour over the vegetables. Cover and refrigerate overnight in the bowl or transfer to a 1-gallon resealable plastic bag. If you transfer to a bag, you may want to keep the bag in a bowl to prevent spills.

2 The pickles and liquid can be transferred to jars or stay in the resealable plastic bag. They will keep in the fridge for about a week.

HAM SALAD

Grandmama's ham salad created such a taste impression or food memory on me as a child that I feel the urge to re-create it even when I don't have leftover ham. She never wrote this recipe down, either, so this is my best shot at it. I often call my mother to ask her exactly what Grandmama did or how much of something *she* puts in, and usually her response is, "You're going to have to come over and watch me." So many gifted cooks just do what they do without even *knowing* what they are doing!

This "salad" is less like a meal or side dish and more like a spread, a Southern pâté that's delicious on crackers and especially on a biscuit. When I do get that craving and I don't have or need a whole ham, I ask the butcher to cut some ham in thicker slabs rather than slices for sandwiches.

Makes 4 cups, enough for 8 sandwiches

1 pound ham (leftover or purchased thick slab), trimmed and diced
½ cup chopped onion
3 stalks celery, chopped
2 dill "sandwich-sliced" pickles, chopped

⅔ cup mayonnaise
2 tablespoons Dijon mustard
1 tablespoon light brown sugar
1½ teaspoons pickle juice
Kosher salt and freshly ground black pepper

1 Put the ham, onion, and celery in a food processor. Pulse 20 to 25 times to mince. Remove to a bowl and mix in the remaining ingredients. Chill. Taste and adjust the salt and pepper before serving.
2 Serve on sandwiches, crackers, or cheese biscuits or mix into the yolk mixture of deviled eggs.

Note: Adjust the amount of mayonnaise and salt depending on the saltiness of the ham and the desired consistency of the salad.

AVOCADO MAYO BLTS

This sandwich, whose ingredients you can easily pack separately to keep fresh, makes a great picnic/dock/boat/beach meal. You'll need only a little assembly when you're ready to eat.

Cook the bacon ahead of time, let it cool, and wrap in plastic. Peel (see page 157) and slice tomatoes ahead and wrap or put in a Tupperware container. Do the same for pieces of washed and dried lettuce. Premix a little kosher salt and freshly cracked pepper together in a small Tupperware container, and store the avocado mayo in a small Tupperware container as well. Toss all these in a larger container that can go in a cooler, tote along a loaf of bread and a knife for spreading the mayo, and impress your friends when you pull out all the ingredients for fantastic fresh sandwiches. No more soggy PB&Js or flat ham-and-cheeses!

Makes 1 cup spread, enough for 8 to 12 sandwiches

½ cup mayonnaise
½ avocado, pitted, peeled, and diced
3 tablespoons minced red onion
2 tablespoons fresh basil cut in chiffonade (see page 219)

½ teaspoon fresh lemon juice
Kosher salt and freshly ground black pepper
Tomatoes, peeled (see page 157) and sliced

Toasted bread
Bacon
Lettuce

1 Combine the mayonnaise, avocado, onion, basil, lemon juice, 1 teaspoon salt, and pepper to taste, smashing the avocado with a fork to incorporate. Chill in the fridge for the flavors to marry until ready to assemble the sandwiches.
2 Sprinkle the tomatoes with salt and pepper. Spread the avocado mayo on bread slices. Assemble the sandwiches with bacon, lettuce, and tomato. Have extra napkins on hand!

FIERY PIMENTO CHEESE–LACED
"NAUGHTY" EGGS

John, my husband, loves deviled eggs. I tried to make myself like them, but I just never did. Until I added pimento cheese. Now I crave them, too, and they are part of our regular summertime repertoire. Everyone attacks these eggs, and when we make plans with friends, they often ask, "Can you make those deviled eggs again?" These are so good, they are worth buying one of those Tupperware containers that have the oval divots to hold the eggs in. We pop our egg container in the cooler with the drinks and take them out in the boat with us for a filling snack.

My daughter Cate usually eats one too many of these at a time, but at least she is getting her protein. I also get excited when my girls like spicy foods—I'm training their palates to like all kinds of foods and flavors. Naughty eggs for good girls!

Makes 24 deviled eggs

12 eggs
½ cup mayonnaise
¾ cup spicy pimento cheese
Kosher salt and freshly ground black pepper
Garnishes (optional): ⅓ cup thinly sliced green onions, chopped pimento

1 Boil, cook, and peel the eggs (see Perfectly Peeled Boiled Eggs, below).
2 Cut the eggs in half lengthwise. Remove the yolks and place in a bowl. Place the whites on a platter or in a Tupperware deviled egg container.
3 Add the mayonnaise and pimento cheese to the yolks. Season with salt and pepper. Fluff with a fork. Spoon into a resealable plastic bag, cut off one corner of the bag, and pipe the yolk mixture into the centers of the whites.
4 Garnish with green onions or pimento, if you wish.

Perfectly Peeled Boiled Eggs

For most purposes, you can boil eggs as directed in the recipe for Hudson's Egg Salad (page 118), but for deviled eggs, it's especially crucial to have a peeled egg without any bumps, divots, or rips. Mike Lata, the chef at FIG, one of my very favorite restaurants in Charleston, shared his method with my mother, and she and I have been using it ever since. This meticulous approach is worth the effort when presentation is important.

Before boiling, take a needle or thumbtack and gently prick one end of each egg. Put the eggs in cold water in the pot you'll cook them in and then bring to a boil for 14 minutes. Drain and cool in an ice bath for about 5 minutes, or until the eggs are cool enough to touch. Peel the eggs under water for beautiful, smooth-skinned eggs.

Condolence Food

When someone passes away in the South, the body hasn't left the house before people are dropping by with food for the family. Food is an essential way that Southerners celebrate and connect with one another and it's also a way we communicate the unspeakable to each other, the way we try to show our sympathy for those going through sorrow and loss when words are not sufficient. It's one thing when someone has lived a long and happy life and the gatherings around the person's death include telling stories about his or her misadventures and repeating all the lines he or she was famous for saying. But it's another when tragedy happens without any sign of a silver lining or any clear reason to believe it was meant to be.

When I was newly married, my friends Allie and Jerrod had a baby boy, Hudson, who died shortly after birth. It was a terrible shock for them and for all of us. I called my mother and asked, "What do I do? What do I say?" And she said, "You go over there and get in that kitchen and do what you do." So I fixed some egg salad and picked up a loaf of bread and went over to Allie's. I really didn't say much, but I made egg salad sandwiches, wrote down who brought what on a list so Allie could thank them later, kept track of people's serving dishes, put out the food people brought over, picked up plates and glasses, and washed dishes. I simply tried to keep the kitchen going, food at the ready, and drinks flowing for the family and friends who gathered to mourn and comfort one another. Food is so much more than sustenance. It's a way of caring, comforting, and supporting, holding up friends and family just a little when they'd rather crumble.

There is hidden power in the food you take to somebody going through something terrible. It is a little bit of fuel to help them make it through their ordeal. It's one less thing for their burdened mind to worry about—whether it's feeding themselves or their children or their guests. It's a message saying that you acknowledge their pain, that you are there for them, that you are thinking of them, and that if you could do anything in the world that would help ease their anguish, they just need to tell you what that is and you will do it in a skinny minute.

There's no way to keep people in the South from coming by when there's a death in the family. It's in our blood to surround those who are hurting with food and love. And you better have the food and drinks ready—even though most people bring things, there are always a few who make you wonder if they are simply there for the food. A friend of mine told me of a family funeral where someone brought plastic bags to take food home with her! Here are some good ideas for things to take over to a family in mourning so that they have plenty for themselves and to serve those who drop by.

Egg salad and bread for sandwiches (page 118)

Chicken salad and bread or rolls for sandwiches (page 110)

Ham salad and biscuits (page 112)

Warm fried chicken (page 62) with a side of potato salad (page 133)
or cole slaw (page 132)

"Naughty" eggs (page 114)

Spread from DILLicious Cucumber Sandwiches as a dip
with crudités (page 108)

Tuna casserole (page 233)

Cookies (page 168)

Pitchers or jugs of fresh iced tea (page 242) or lemonade (page 239)

A cooler full of cold beer

Bottles of wine

A bottle of vodka accompanied by Bloody Mary mix or fresh fruit juices
such as orange and grapefruit

Pitcher of premixed Salty Dog Vodka Soda with limes and grapefruit slices
(page 236)

HUDSON'S EGG SALAD

*Makes enough for 8 sandwiches,
or 6 to 8 servings of salad*

12 eggs
¾ cup minced onion
½ to ¾ cup mayonnaise
1 tablespoon Dijon mustard
½ teaspoon fresh lemon juice

½ teaspoon hot sauce
¼ teaspoon Worcestershire sauce
Kosher salt and freshly ground
   black pepper

Garnish for sandwiches
   (optional): Finely chopped
   fresh herbs

1 Place the eggs in a saucepan large enough to hold them. Cover with cold water by 1 to 2 inches. Place over medium heat and bring just to boil; you will see the bubbles rising around the pot, but the water is not at a roll. Reduce the heat to simmer and cook 6 minutes. Remove from the heat, cover, and let sit 10 minutes.

2 Drain the eggs and place in a bowl of ice water until cold.
3 Drain the water and roll the eggs around to crack the whole surface. Begin peeling at the large end. It helps to peel them under cold running water.
4 Place the eggs in a large bowl and mash with a fork. Stir in the remaining ingredients. Adjust the salt, pepper, and mayonnaise to your taste.

5 Optional, if using for sandwiches: Spread the herbs on a plate. Press the sides of each sandwich into the herbs so that the herbs stick to the egg salad between the bread slices. Makes for a pretty presentation.

TUNA THREE WAYS

CLASSIC TUNA FISH SALAD

Makes 6 servings

We eat so much tuna fish, I buy it in bulk. I like it and John and our girls do, too, thank goodness. I put the following three varieties on sandwiches, on crackers, and sometimes simply on top of greens as a salad—great versatility for when you want to make a bunch ahead of time and use it as needed for a flexible summer schedule.

3 (5-ounce) cans water-packed albacore tuna, chilled and drained
½ cup minced white onion
⅓ cup diced celery
½ cup mayonnaise
3 tablespoons sweet pickle relish
¾ to 1 teaspoon kosher salt
½ teaspoon freshly ground black pepper

1 Put the tuna in a medium bowl and use a fork to break it up. Stir in the remaining ingredients. Cover and refrigerate for 20 minutes.
2 Taste and adjust the salt and pepper.

TUSCAN TUNA SALAD WITH WHITE BEANS

For best flavor, prepare a few hours before serving.

Makes 4 to 6 servings

BEANS
2 (15.5-ounce) cans high-quality cannellini or
   other white beans, drained and rinsed
2 cloves garlic, minced
2 tablespoons fresh lemon juice
3 tablespoons olive oil
⅓ cup fresh whole flat-leaf parsley leaves
½ teaspoon kosher salt
¼ teaspoon freshly ground black pepper

TUNA
2 (5-ounce) cans water-packed light tuna, drained
½ cup thinly sliced red onion
2 tablespoons olive oil
2 tablespoons red wine vinegar
¼ teaspoon kosher salt
⅛ teaspoon freshly ground black pepper

Garnish (optional): Chopped cherry tomatoes

1 Make the beans: In a medium bowl, combine all
the ingredients. Set aside to allow the flavors to
marry.
2 Make the tuna: In another bowl, flake the tuna
with a fork to break up the pieces. Stir in the
remaining ingredients. Taste and adjust the salt
and pepper.
3 Combine the beans and tuna, cover, and chill.

SOHO TUNA SALAD

Makes 6 servings

3 (5-ounce) cans water-packed albacore tuna,
   drained
¼ cup plus 2 tablespoons mayonnaise
¼ cup minced red onion
1 tablespoon nonpareil capers in brine, drained
¼ cup minced carrots
2 teaspoons fresh lemon juice, or more to taste
3 tablespoons snipped fresh dill
½ to ¾ teaspoon kosher salt
¼ teaspoon freshly ground black pepper

In a medium bowl, break up the tuna with a fork.
Stir in the remaining ingredients. Taste and adjust
the salt and pepper, as capers contribute a salty
flavor. Cover and chill.

SUMMER CRAB SALAD
WITH GREEN
"PRINCESSES" DRESSING

Crabbing is one of our favorite summertime activities, and I put together this recipe after introducing crabbing to my friend Claire and her family, who live in London and come to Charleston twice a year. Claire has two girls, Isla and Maisie, very close in age to my three, and the five girls make quite the crabbing team. Our crab lines consist of string wrapped around whatever kind of stick we happen to have or find. We tie a raw chicken neck (the further past the sell-by date, the better!) to the end of the string as bait. We toss the necks off a dock (usually my mother's) into a saltwater creek, holding on to the sticks or tying them off on a dock cleat. Then we check each line for the twitching and tugging

1 pound freshly caught and
   picked crabmeat, or 1
   (16-ounce) container fresh lump
   crabmeat
1 teaspoon fresh lemon juice
2 large avocados, pitted, peeled,
   and diced
2 tomatoes, cored, seeded, and
   diced
2 green onions, thinly sliced
   (white and green parts)
⅓ cup fresh chives snipped with
   kitchen shears
⅓ cup fresh dill snipped with
   kitchen shears
Green "Princesses" Dressing
   (recipe follows)
Kosher salt and freshly ground
   black pepper

1 Gently go through the crabmeat with your fingers, feeling for and removing any hard shell or cartilage pieces.
2 Place the crabmeat in a chilled bowl and sprinkle with the lemon juice. Add the avocados, tomatoes, green onions, chives, and dill and toss gently to combine.
3 Fold in the dressing to taste and season with salt and pepper. Cover and chill before serving.

Green "Princesses" Dressing

Makes about 1¼ cups

1 cup mayonnaise
1 small cucumber, peeled,
   seeded, and chopped (I prefer
   the seedless English variety, but
   any variety is fine)
2 green onions, chopped (white
   and green parts)
2 cups coarsely chopped mixed
   fresh herbs (chives, dill, flat-leaf
   parsley, cilantro)

3 or 4 small cloves garlic,
   coarsely chopped
2 tablespoons olive oil
2 teaspoons white wine vinegar
¾ to 1 teaspoon anchovy paste
Kosher salt and freshly ground
   black pepper

Place the ingredients in a mini food processor or blender and puree. Taste and adjust the salt and pepper. Any leftover dressing can be stored in the fridge in a covered container for up to 3 days.

of a crab biting on the chicken neck. (And that day a crab on the line was announced by Isla's and Maisie's beautiful accents exclaiming, "Brilliant! I've got one! I've got one!") One person pulls in the line inch by inch, super slowly so the crab comes up with the chicken neck and doesn't let go. Another person stands ready with the net to scoop up the crab from behind before the crab notices anything and lets go. When we have enough, we clean the crabs, steam them, put down plenty of newspaper on the table, and pick the crabs of all their meat, sneaking bites of fresh crabmeat every now and then.

Canned crabmeat works okay for this recipe, but if you can find a tub of fresh-picked crab, it's better. And if you catch your own crab, you know nothing tastes better than the fruit of your own "labor." I was craving something cool and creamy that day to put on the salad, but I didn't have all the ingredients for a traditional green goddess dressing, so I improvised and found I liked the outcome better than the original. I usually end up using whatever herbs I happen to have on hand—in fact, this dressing is probably a little different every time I make it. Since it's not exactly a classic green goddess, I call it green "princesses" after my girls, who love it!

Makes 4 servings

I love fried okra. It's on my "last meal" list. My children don't love okra yet, but I try to sneak it in and add it to everything, and most of the time it works. In this salad, the fried okra is like croutons. The okra does have to be cooked, but you can make it ahead of time—it doesn't need to be served hot on the salad. Especially in the summer, you may want to do the frying in the morning when the temperature is a little cooler.

Texture is everything in this salad—crispy okra, smooth, creamy goat cheese, nutty pepitas. Add a very chilled white wine and this makes the perfect summer evening meal.

Makes 6 servings

FRIED OKRA AND PEPITA SALAD

1 pound okra, ends trimmed, chopped
½ cup diced white onion
⅛ teaspoon cayenne pepper, or more to taste
½ teaspoon kosher salt

¼ teaspoon freshly ground black pepper
1 or 2 tablespoons butter
1 or 2 tablespoons olive oil, or more if needed
2 heads Bibb lettuce

¼ to ⅓ cup roasted and salted pepitas (pumpkin seeds)
2 ounces soft goat cheese
Vinaigrette of your choice, such as those on pages 127 and 131

1 Mix together the okra, onion, cayenne, salt, and pepper in a bowl and let sit for a few minutes for the flavors to marry.
2 Melt 1 tablespoon of butter into 1 tablespoon of olive oil in a cast-iron skillet on medium to high heat. Add the okra-onion mixture and spread in a single layer; do not overcrowd. (You will probably need to cook the okra in 2 batches unless you are using a large skillet.) Let the okra cook undisturbed for about 10 minutes.
3 Turn the okra to brown the other side, about 10 minutes more. (The key to fried okra is to not stir or fuss with it, so it gets crispy.) Once the okra is brown and crisp, remove to a paper bag to remove the excess grease.
4 Tear the leaves from 1 head of lettuce into bite-size pieces; place in a salad bowl, and add the pepitas. Pinch off pea-size pieces of goat cheese and add to the salad. Toss in the fried okra, cover, and refrigerate.
5 When you're ready to serve, divide the other head of lettuce onto 6 plates, using the biggest leaves. Toss the salad with vinaigrette and place on the prepared plates.

COLLARD AND BRUSSELS SPROUTS SALAD

My childhood friend Krysten has lived in California for fifteen years. That distance has not caused our friendship to fade one bit. Talking on the phone about cooking is how we stay connected. It's also how we connect in person. When we get together, food and drinks are always part of our agenda.

As a Southern transplant in California, Krysten is always introducing her West Coast friends to Southern cooking. In this recipe, she takes collards, a Southern staple, and prepares it in a fresh California salad rather than cooking it slowly as we would in the South. Krysten is a super-talented cook, and I love the way this recipe represents her bicoastal sensibility and our friendship that's been able to thrive cross country, as well.

Makes 6 servings

1 cup pecan pieces
6 to 8 slices thick-cut bacon, diced (about 1 cup)
1½ pounds collard greens, stems removed

12 ounces Brussels sprouts, shaved or sliced paper thin
1 cup grated Parmesan cheese
Mustard Vinaigrette Dressing (page 127)

Kosher salt and freshly ground black pepper

1 Preheat the oven to 325°F. Spread the pecans on a baking sheet and toast for 6 to 8 minutes. Let cool.
2 Cook the bacon in a skillet until browned and crispy. Remove to a paper bag to drain and cool. (Save the drippins for another use.)

3 Cut the collards into very thin strips with a very sharp knife or pulse in a food processor until finely chopped. Remove to a large bowl. Add the Brussels sprouts, pecans, bacon, and Parmesan. Toss with the dressing.

4 Let the salad rest in the fridge for about 3 minutes. Taste and season with salt and pepper before serving.

Note: Bacon Vinaigrette (page 131) also works well with this salad.

MUSTARD VINAIGRETTE DRESSING

Makes about ½ cup

1 teaspoon Dijon mustard
¾ teaspoon honey
1 tablespoon fresh lemon juice
¼ cup sherry vinegar
¼ cup extra virgin olive oil
½ teaspoon kosher salt
Freshly ground black pepper

Whisk together all the ingredients.

My stepmother, Caroline, spent all of her childhood summers on a 1,400-acre ranch in Madeira, California, settled by her great-grandfather in the 1870s. Growing up, I always spent a few weeks of every summer there. Caroline's Aunt Brookie and cousin Celia still farm Mordecai Ranch, which is now planted with almond groves. From the highway to the main house is a beautiful drive lined and shaded by towering eucalyptus trees—the Western version of an avenue of live oaks on a Southern plantation. Another similarity to the South is the hot weather! It is less humid there and it does get cooler at night, but during the day, temperatures reach 120 degrees and there is no air conditioning. You end up craving cold foods just like you do in the South and avoid turning on a hot oven or stove at all costs.

Chilling the bowl ahead of time for this salad may be the most brilliant idea ever, and I think it needs to be immediately adopted as a new Southern tradition.

Makes 4 servings

CELIA'S AVOCADO AND CUCUMBER SALAD

1 large salad cucumber, scrubbed but unpeeled
1 large avocado
3 or 4 green onions, chopped (white and green parts)

¼ cup roasted, salted sunflower seeds
Kosher salt and freshly ground black pepper

Vinaigrette of your choice (see page 131)

1 Chill the salad bowl.
2 Cut the cucumber lengthwise in quarters. Use a spoon to scoop out the seeds. Cut the quarters in ¼-inch-thick slices.

Pit, peel, and slice the avocado ¼ inch thick. Cut the slices in half.
3 Place the cucumber, avocado, green onions, and sunflower seeds in the bowl and toss to combine. Season with salt and pepper. Add dressing to taste and toss again.

When I think of "salad," this is what I think of. The recipe includes cucumbers, bell peppers, and tomatoes, but to be honest I love it just as much with lettuce as the only vegetable. The preparation, albeit incredibly simple, is so unique and flavorful that the salad doesn't require further adornment. Mashing up the garlic and salt is a ritual that makes my mouth water with anticipation, and then when the salad is chilling in the refrigerator, I savor the aroma of garlicky goodness that comes wafting out every time I open the refrigerator door. This is a staple to be learned by heart and repeated multiple times a week.

Makes 4 servings

GRANDMAMA'S GREEN DINNER SALAD

1 teaspoon kosher salt
1 large clove garlic
Freshly ground black pepper
1 cup peeled, seeded, and chopped cucumber (I prefer the seedless English variety, but any variety will work)

½ cup chopped green bell pepper
½ cup chopped red bell pepper
½ cup chopped seeded tomatoes
4 cups chopped romaine lettuce

1 tablespoon good-quality extra virgin olive oil
1 tablespoon good-quality red wine vinegar

1 Place the salt and garlic in a salad bowl. Use the back of a fork to mash them together to form a paste. Grind about 8 turns of the pepper mill over the paste and mix well. Spread the paste over the inside of the bowl. Layer the vegetables in the bowl, ending with the lettuce. Refrigerate 1 hour.

2 Drizzle with the olive oil and vinegar. Toss, adjust the salt and pepper, and serve.

VINAIGRETTE VARIATIONS

Makes about 1 cup each

For the balsamic, lemon, and lime vinaigrettes, combine all the ingredients in a jar. Cap tightly and shake to blend. Let mellow 5 minutes. Taste and adjust the salt and pepper. Shake well again before using.

BALSAMIC VINAIGRETTE

⅓ cup balsamic vinegar
1 clove garlic, minced
2 tablespoons minced shallots or onions
1 tablespoon fresh lemon juice
⅔ cup extra virgin olive oil
Kosher salt and freshly ground black pepper

LEMON VINAIGRETTE

¾ cup vegetable oil
⅓ cup fresh lemon juice
2 teaspoons grated lemon zest
½ to 1 teaspoon Dijon mustard
½ to ¾ teaspoon kosher salt

LIME VINAIGRETTE

¾ cup vegetable oil
⅓ cup fresh lime juice
2 teaspoons grated lime zest
½ to 1 teaspoon Dijon mustard
½ to ¾ teaspoon kosher salt

BACON VINAIGRETTE

4 slices bacon
1 large shallot, minced
¼ cup white wine vinegar or red wine vinegar
Juice of ½ lemon
½ cup extra virgin olive oil
2 tablespoons chopped fresh flat-leaf parsley
Kosher salt and freshly ground black pepper

1 Cook the bacon in a skillet until crispy. Leaving the drippins in the pan, remove the bacon to a paper bag to drain and cool. Chop and reserve for garnish.
2 Cook the shallot in the drippins 3 to 5 minutes, stirring occasionally, until soft.
3 Combine the vinegar, lemon juice, olive oil, and parsley in a jar. Add the shallot and drippins. Cap tightly and shake well. Taste and season with salt and black pepper if needed.
4 If the dressing congeals, place the jar in a bowl of warm water until it pours.

CHILDHOOD SOUTHERN COLE SLAW

Life lesson: Always write down your recipes. I would give anything to have a direct line to Grandmama so I could ask her once and for all what she put in her slaw. I have spent years trying different tweaks to this recipe to replicate the flavor of her original. I have my mother to thank for the addition of the green olives that she puts in her version of it. When I was little, I craved green olives with everything. At restaurants I'd order water or Sprite—with green olives! There is something about the salty flavor I have always loved. This recipe is delicious, and it combines my best attempt at Grandmama's original with Callie's green olive addition, a true blend of the generations. But I'd chuck it all for the slaw of my childhood!

Makes 8 servings

1 head cabbage (2½ to 3 pounds), sliced super thin
3 teaspoons celery seeds
2½ teaspoons kosher salt

⅓ cup cider vinegar
Ice water
1 cup mayonnaise
2 tablespoons white vinegar

1 tablespoon mustard seeds
½ teaspoon cayenne pepper
1½ cups sliced green olives

1 In a large container, combine the cabbage with 2 teaspoons of the celery seeds, 2 teaspoons of salt, the cider vinegar, and ice water to cover. Refrigerate overnight.

2 Drain well. Place in a large bowl. Combine the mayonnaise, white vinegar, mustard seeds, cayenne, and the remaining ½ teaspoon salt and 1 teaspoon celery seeds. Add to the cabbage and mix well. Gently fold in the olives. Refrigerate until chilled.

Q'S POTATO SALAD

Q is Quincy, my mother's best friend and, after my mother and stepmother, a third mother to me. She knows what she wants when she wants it how she wants it. She does not sugarcoat anything, and she has no problem telling me like it is. At the same time, she is my greatest cheerleader and a very important person in my life. I used to babysit her daughters, and now they babysit mine. I don't think I'll ever outgrow needing her wisdom. Not only is she a beautiful person inside and out, but she is a fabulous cook. I can't get enough of her, and I can never get enough of her potato salad. Serve this with fried chicken and sliced fresh tomatoes for a perfect summer supper.

Makes 6 servings

5 to 6 medium red skin potatoes
Kosher salt
1 cup mayonnaise
1 tablespoon tangy mustardy
  sandwich spread
1 to 2 teaspoons all-purpose
  Greek seasoning

1 teaspoon freshly ground black
  pepper
½ cup finely chopped sweet
  onion (Vidalia if in season)
1 cup diced celery
2 kosher dill pickles, chopped
  (not pickle relish)

1 teaspoon white vinegar
Optional: 2 boiled eggs, peeled
  and chopped
Garnish (optional): Snipped fresh
  dill or paprika

1 Peel the potatoes and cut in quarters. Place in a saucepan and cover with cold water. Add 2 teaspoons salt. Bring to a boil, cover, and reduce the heat to medium. Cook 8 minutes.
2 Use the tip of a knife to check for tenderness. Drain if done, or cook 2 to 4 minutes more if needed, but do not overcook. Drain well and place in a bowl.

3 Combine the mayonnaise, sandwich spread, Greek seasoning, the pepper, and ½ teaspoon salt. Stir gently into the warm potatoes. Let sit at least 30 minutes.
4 In a separate bowl, combine the onion, celery, pickles, vinegar, and salt to taste.
5 If you are serving the potato salad at room temperature, add the onion mixture 30 minutes

before serving. If you are serving the potato salad cold, chill the potato salad and when cold, add the onion mixture.
6 Fold in the eggs just before serving, if using. If you like, sprinkle the finished salad with dill or paprika.

This is my mother, Callie's, creation. It is a little bit like a Southwestern version of succotash. It's fresh and clean tasting, a simply irresistible combination of flavors that takes corn and elevates it to a whole other level. We are lucky enough to have tons of fresh corn in the South, and this is a fantastic alternative to corn on the cob. It's also incredibly versatile. The addition of the avocado makes it a meal in itself. You can serve it at room temperature alongside pork loin for a fancy dish or alongside BBQ chicken from the grill. Or serve it chilled as a dip with tortilla chips. It can keep in the fridge for days. Do be sure, though, not to add the avocados until just before serving.

Makes 6 to 8 cups

SUMMER CORN SALAD

8 ears corn, shucked
2 red bell peppers, seeded and diced
1 cup loosely packed fresh cilantro leaves

½ red onion, diced
½ to 1 teaspoon kosher salt
¼ teaspoon freshly ground black pepper
1 tablespoon olive oil

2 teaspoons grated lime zest
Juice of 2 limes, plus more if needed
2 avocados, pitted, peeled, and diced

1 Steam or boil the corn until tender.
2 Cool the corn in ice water. Drain and dry well. Use a large knife to cut the kernels from the cobs.

3 Combine the bell peppers, cilantro, and onion in a large bowl. Add the corn. Season with the salt and pepper and stir in the olive oil and lime zest and juice. Cover and chill to allow the flavors to marry.
4 Taste and adjust for salt and lime juice. Fold in the avocados and serve.

FROZEN FRUIT KEBOBS

One summer, my friend Wyche and I went with my mother and stepfather to Nantucket to babysit my little brothers who were one and two at the time. Wyche and I were rising high school seniors and were absolutely taken by the beautiful men walking along the surf singing out, "King Kebobs, King Kebobs!" and selling delicious skewers of frozen fruit. The hunks, the beauty of Nantucket, and the kebobs all made a huge impression on me, and I ended up returning to Nantucket for three summers during college, working at an all-girls' full-service Mobil gas station as what we employees liked to call a "petroleum transfer engineer." Best job ever!

I like to make my own "Queen Kebobs" and take them from the freezer to the boat cooler. They do defrost a little in the cooler, but out on the boat all that drippy goodness is easily washed away with a swim. And for an adult boat trip, I marinate the fruit in vodka before freezing to add a little Nantucket indulgence to this perfect chilly treat.

Makes 12 servings

Your choice of mixed fruit: strawberries, grapes, blueberries, pineapple, watermelon
1½ cups vodka
Grated zest of 1 lemon

1 Cut pineapple and melon into chunks. You'll need about 6 dozen pieces of fruit, total.
2 For a nonalcoholic version, thread 6 to 10 pieces of fruit onto each skewer, wrap in clear plastic wrap, and freeze.
3 For an adult version, put the vodka and lemon zest in a large resealable plastic bag. Add the fruit. Let marinate in the fridge for a few hours. Skewer the marinated fruit, about 6 to 10 pieces per skewer. Wrap in plastic wrap and freeze.
4 For another adult variation, marinate in Morey Margarita (page 238) instead of vodka and lemon zest. Skewer and wrap the same way.

Note: If making alcoholic and nonalcoholic kebobs at the same time, wrap the nonalcoholic ones in colored plastic wrap to avoid a mix-up!

On the Boat "Dining"

In the Lowcountry, you don't have to have a lot of money to have a boat or have a friend with a boat. There are certainly those with big fancy boats and fast motors, but there are also plenty of the aluminum boats we call john boats, old boats with cushions patched with duct tape, and boats that hold a lot of people and a lot of fun but don't go all that fast. In other words, the water is a summer destination for almost everyone. One of our favorite boating locales is Rockville, where my Uncle Jimmy and Aunt Gail host Easter and tree golf. Uncle Jimmy and Aunt Gail have a little house made out of oyster tabby ("Southern stucco," or concrete mixed with oyster shells). There's a kitchen on the ground floor and two bedrooms on the second floor—one bedroom is the girls' side and the other is the boys' side. The sexes are split, with each sleeping in its designated bunkroom—even married couples must separate for the night! The only big part of the house is the screened porch.

My father and stepmother now have a small home on the property, and we spend time there going back and forth between the two houses and sitting on the porches, but mostly we go out in the boat on Adams Creek for hours at a time. That's one reason why such small cottages work even when the whole family is together—besides the porches, we really only use the houses to sleep in. The rest of the time we are out in the creek!

Unlike the lake where planning the menu is part of the fun, the focus at Rockville is less on eating and, for the adults, a little more on drinking—in moderation, of course! So snacks accompany us everywhere, and they need to be snacks that are easy to tote, stow in the cooler, and pull out as needed. Here are a few of our favorite totable boat snacks. Tupperware containers help!

Mom's Perfect Tomato Sandwiches (page 107)

Sandwiches with Ham Salad (page 112)

DILLicious Cucumber Sandwiches (page 108)

Sandwiches with Tuna Three Ways (page 120)

"Naughty" Eggs (see page 114)

Boiled Peanuts (page 218)

Dad's No-Recipe Shrimp (page 140)

Frozen Fruit Kebobs (page 136)

Summer Corn Salad (page 135) as a dip with tortilla chips

Lime Berry Cooler (page 238)

Watermelon wedges

Dad's No Recipe Shrimp

When I was little, shrimping was a part of most weekends during the shrimp season. Dad's boat, the *Rainbow Runner*, had sparkly rainbow stripes along the sides. Sometimes I would go out with him, and one day we were putting the boat in the water at the Shem Creek boat landing, the busiest boat landing in town. The boat was on a trailer behind my grandfather's old green wood-paneled station wagon, and Dad was backing it down the ramp into the water, when the wagon's brakes gave out. The boat and the station wagon with it rolled right into Shem Creek and sank, putting a real wrench in the plans of the other boaters who were lined up for their turn to use the ramp. The station wagon and boat were towed out and put back into working condition, but for weeks and weeks, several times over, as soon as we'd decide the old station wagon had finally dried out, a little more water would drain out from its recesses.

Dad and his next-door neighbor Paul Simmons continue to go out on a boat together, though the *Rainbow Runner* is no longer with us, and throw the cast net for shrimp and stock their freezers with enough to get themselves through the off season. Open my father's refrigerator any time of day any time of year and there will be a porcelain bowl full of "bull shrimp," as my father pronounces "boiled shrimp" in his Lowcountry accent. He also likes to put the cold "bull shrimp" in a resealable plastic bag, put the bag in the cooler, and take it out in the boat. We peel the shrimp as we eat, tossing the shells overboard into the water.

When I asked him how he fixes his shrimp, assuming there would be some kind of secret method or some seasoning involved, this is what he told me: "You don't put anything on those. Soon as you put them in the pot and soon as they turn pink, you take them out. They taste perfectly good without any of that."

To translate, here's Dad's "no-recipe" method for "bull shrimp":

Head the shrimp if they aren't already headed. Bring a pot of water to a boil. Add the shrimp. Boil just until pink, about 2 minutes. Drain in a colander. Chill in the fridge. Serve cold, peeling the shrimp as you eat them.

Do keep in mind that one reason why Dad's shrimp don't need any seasoning is that the shrimp are super fresh and right out of the cast net. So try to get the freshest shrimp available. Otherwise, get out the Old Bay!

BAKING

My earliest memory of baking takes me back to Mama's kitchen and the sound of her old worn tin sifter. She sifted everything, even cake mixes from the box. I can still hear the tiny squeak of the sifter handle and the *fwoot fwoot fwoot* sound of the wire scraping against the mesh. I wish that I could transport my girls back to Mama's kitchen so they could hear her sweet voice and help her make some of the "haystack cookies" she would always make for me out of butterscotch chips and crunchy noodles. The girls and I sat down not to long ago and went through Mama's three recipe file boxes—one and a half of which were full of desserts! That tells you just how strong her sweet tooth was. I couldn't help but hold the recipe cards up to my nose and soak up the smell of her kitchen and rub my fingers over her handwriting as if it might take us all there in a cloud of flour.

I figure the best way I can take my girls to Mama's kitchen is to keep making her favorite recipes, telling them stories about her, and showing them how she did things. Going through her recipe boxes was exploring a treasure trove, and as we read the names of the recipes out loud and talked about which ones we wanted to make, we tried to figure out by the stains and wear on the cards which ones she had used the most. It was like finding the most precious gems among the bunch. The cards for Sour Cream Banana Pudding, Praline Squares, German Chocolate Cake, and Fruit Cake seemed to be the most well loved, and we are now on a mission to re-create those and as many more of her jewels as possible.

As simple and straightforward as most of Mama's recipes are, I was always too intimidated to try her homemade piecrust. Until, that is, I started making biscuits. To me, homemade piecrust had the same connotation in my mind as making homemade biscuits: complicated, requiring meticulous measurements and handling, and easy to mess up. But making piecrust is so similar to making biscuits. If you are just starting to make biscuits, start making piecrusts, too. The way you handle the dough is very similar. And, like the biscuits, you can master it; you will get better the more times you do it, and it's so good that even if it's not perfect your first few times, it will still taste great. Just like the biscuits, trust the butter and the flour to cover all sins!

Below are a few other piecrust tips I've picked up along the way that will make your piecrust making much more enjoyable.

HAND MIX THE DOUGH. Sound familiar, biscuit makers? Flour your hands so the dough is not too sticky and work the butter into the flour so it gets that same consistency as grated Parmesan cheese.

USE GOOD FLOUR. AND A TON OF IT! Either use a high-quality all-purpose flour such as White Lily or use cake flour. This is the main ingredient of the crust, so it's got to be good. Also be sure to generously flour all of the surfaces you are working on so the dough doesn't stick.

MAKE SURE INGREDIENTS ARE COLD. The butter and the water must be cold to get the consistency and texture of the crust just right.

USE PARCHMENT PAPER. Flour it generously, roll out the dough on it, and use it to move the dough where you need it.

WORK QUICKLY. Otherwise, your ingredients will warm up and the dough will get too elastic.

ROLL IT. Roll from the center of the dough outward rather than back and forth. Roll out the dough larger than the pie dish.

DOUBLE IT. This way you can use one crust now and freeze one for later—how nice to be able to whip up a fresh galette or pie any time you feel like it or any time you need a quick dessert.

MAKE A TOP CRUST. To make a top crust for your pie, double the recipe. Roll the bottom crust onto the parchment paper larger than the top crust, as the bottom has to cover the larger area lining the pan. In order to transfer the crust to the pie dish, you can wrap the dough onto a well-floured rolling pin, peel off the exposed sheet of parchment paper, unroll the dough into the bottom of the pie dish or onto the top of the pie (depending on whether it's the top or the bottom crust), and remove the other sheet of parchment paper.

PRACTICE. I'm not a patient person, but I've gotten piecrust down pat, and you will, too. You can patch up holes when you need to, and if you do feel like throwing away a batch of dough and starting over, so be it! The ingredients are inexpensive, and you probably have plenty of these staples on hand anyway. Don't think too hard about it—just start doing it.

CARRIE'S TIPS

Cake Flour I get my love of cake flour from Mama. The red box with the swan hasn't changed since I saw it on her kitchen counter as a little girl. She used cake flour a lot of times even when a recipe didn't call for it. It's so soft and feels so good as you work with it in your hands. You can sift it and make it even lighter. To substitute cake flour for all-purpose and vice versa: 1 cup all-purpose flour = 1 cup + 2 tablespoons cake flour.

"Shiny Pans" Southerners go through a lot of those affordable grocery store disposable aluminum pans because we are always taking food with us wherever we go and making food for other people. But the most amazing thing about these pans is that you can cut them up and mold them into any shape you need. I've even taken a rectangular one, bent the sides flat, pinched it together in a seam down the middle, and then rounded up the long sides to make a French loaf pan. Try my Aunt Em's bread (see page 165) this way. If you're out of town and need a certain kind of pan, even a pie dish, take whatever kind of foil pan you have or can find and reshape it. Another opportunity to experiment and another reason why you don't need a lot of fancy equipment to be a great cook.

MAMA'S BUTTER PIECRUST

Makes 1 crust for a 9-inch pie

2¼ cups cake flour or 2 cups all-purpose flour

⅓ teaspoon kosher salt
12 tablespoons (1½ sticks) cold butter, cut in small cubes

5 to 7 tablespoons ice water

1 Mix the flour and the salt. Add the butter and work into the flour with your fingertips just like making biscuits until the mixture has the consistency of grated Parmesan cheese. Mix in the cold water by the tablespoon with your fingers until the dough holds together in a rough ball.
2 Flour a sheet of waxed paper or parchment paper. Dump out the dough onto the paper. Flour the top of the dough and cover with another sheet of paper. Place the whole dough "sandwich" on a baking sheet. Refrigerate 2 hours or overnight.

3 Remove from fridge and leave out for 30 minutes, keeping the dough sandwiched in the paper.
4 With the dough still between the sheets of paper, roll it out to a circle 12 inches in diameter, ¼ inch thick.
5 Peel off the top paper and flip the dough into a 9-inch pie dish.
6 Peel off the other piece of paper. Trim off any extra dough that's hanging over the edge of the pie dish. Press the tines of a fork on the top edge of the crust to crimp it. Fill and bake as the recipe directs.

7 To prebake a crust before filling: Prick the crust in several places with a fork. Chill in the fridge for 30 minutes.
8 Preheat the oven to 400°F.
9 Line the crust with waxed paper and fill with rice or dry beans to add weight. (Save them in a mason jar to reuse the next time. Do not cook them after using for piecrust.) Bake 15 minutes.
10 Remove the waxed paper and weights and bake about 5 to 7 minutes more, until golden brown.
11 Let cool on a rack.

HAYSTACK OR SPIDER COOKIES

Makes 20 to 25 cookies

1 (11-ounce) bag butterscotch chips for haystacks or 1 (10- to 12-ounce) bag chocolate chips for spiders

½ cup chopped pecans
1 (5- to 6-ounce) package crispy chow mein noodles

1 Line a baking sheet with waxed paper.
2 Melt the chips in the top of a double boiler over simmering water. Stir in the pecans. Stir

in the noodles, 1 cup at a time, until covered. (You will need about 3½ cups noodles.) Drop by the heaping tablespoon onto the waxed paper.

3 Refrigerate until hardened. Store in a resealable plastic bag or container for 2 to 3 days or freeze for up to a month.

MAMA'S SOUR CREAM
BANANA PUDDING

Makes 6 to 8 servings

2 (3.4-ounce) packages instant vanilla pudding
2 cups cold milk
1 (8-ounce) container sour cream

1 (8-ounce) container frozen whipped topping
3 to 4 bananas (about 1¾ pounds)

1 (11-ounce) box vanilla wafer cookies

1 Combine the pudding and milk and whisk by hand 2 minutes, or until thickened. Whisk in the sour cream. Set aside ½ cup of the whipped topping and whisk in the rest. Mix well.
2 Cut the bananas into ¼-inch-thick slices.
3 Spread one-third of the pudding in a 2-quart casserole dish. Cover the surface with a layer of wafers, flat side up. Top each wafer with another, rounded side up. Place a banana slice on top of each wafer pair. Fill in the spaces between the cookies with sliced bananas.
4 Repeat with another layer of half of the pudding, wafer pairs, and banana slices.
5 Repeat with the remaining pudding, wafer pairs, and banana slices. Top with the reserved whipped topping.
6 Cover and refrigerate overnight.

Note: Try to purchase name brand ingredients for this recipe rather than generic brands. The better-quality pudding and cookies make a difference.

I love this pie, and I love this story. Alex and I were friends in college and then roommates in New York when I met my husband, John. I give Alex and her pie a good bit of credit for John's and my whirlwind romance. After only two weeks of dating I was ready for John to meet my friends. None of my friends in New York ever had anybody over to their apartments for supper, since we were all single and living in tiny cubbyholes—but I was determined to host a dinner party. I made roast chicken, rice and gravy, and fried okra. Alex said she would make a chess pie. (There are many theories as to the origin of the name "chess pie," but my favorite is that it evolved from people calling it "jes pie," as in "just" a simple pie.)

As we sat finishing up the meal around the grandly set coffee table, Alex went and got the chess pie. When she asked John if he'd like a piece of pie, John said, "No thank you." Well, I wasted no time in kicking him pretty hard under the table. Alex had gone out of her way to make this pie for his visit, and he was being rude not accepting a piece! Later, John told me, "That's the day I knew you were going to be my wife." Apparently he didn't mind and in fact was delighted by a strong-minded woman who would put him in his place when necessary. And he does the same thing to me. Chess pie is now a family tradition John wouldn't dare pass up. And we continue to kick each other under the table—when necessary.

Makes 1 (9-inch) deep-dish pie

ALEX'S
CHOCOLATE CHESS PIE

1 recipe Mama's Butter Piecrust (page 147), prepared and placed in a 9-inch, 2-inch-deep, pie dish
½ pound (2 sticks) butter

2 cups sugar
½ cup unsweetened cocoa powder, sifted
½ cup all-purpose flour
4 large eggs, well beaten

1 teaspoon pure vanilla extract
Serving suggestion: Whipped Cream (page 26) or ice cream

1 Fit the dough into a 9-inch deep-dish pie dish. Trim and crimp the edges.
2 Preheat the oven to 350°F.
3 Melt the butter and pour into a bowl. Add the sugar and mix well. Stir in the cocoa and flour. Add the eggs, mixing well. Stir in the vanilla. Pour into the piecrust. Cover with aluminum foil and bake 45 minutes.
4 Remove the foil and bake 10 to 15 minutes more, until the top stops jiggling and the surface barely moves.
5 Let cool completely on a rack before serving with whipped cream or ice cream.

AUNT FRANCES'S CHOCOLATE
"BONGA" CAKE

Cake making is an art in itself, one I haven't yet mastered. But even I can make this cake without worrying about lopsided layers or the middle caving in. The frosting is a bit more challenging than the cake; its consistency should bring to mind spreadable fudge. John's grand-mother "Bonga" used to make this cake from her sister Frances's recipe, so we lovingly call this moist chocolaty goodness "Bonga Cake" in her memory.

Makes 1 (9 × 13-inch) cake, to serve 12 to 14

CAKE
8 tablespoons (1 stick) butter, plus more for buttering the pan, at room temperature
2 (1-ounce) squares unsweetened chocolate, chopped
1½ cups white sugar
3 large eggs, separated

1 cup buttermilk
1 teaspoon baking soda
2 cups cake flour

FROSTING
½ cup water or coffee
1 cup packed light brown sugar
3 tablespoons butter

3 (1-ounce) squares unsweetened chocolate, chopped
1 tablespoon pure vanilla extract
½ teaspoon kosher salt
1½ to 2 cups powdered sugar, sifted

1 Make the cake: Preheat the oven to 375°F. Butter a 9 × 13-inch baking pan. Melt the chocolate in the top of a double boiler over gently simmering heat. Set aside to cool.
2 Beat the butter with a mixer on medium speed for about 2 minutes. Add the sugar and beat 10 minutes, or until light in color and creamy. Beat in the egg yolks one at a time. Stir in the melted chocolate. Add the buttermilk and mix well.
3 Sift the baking soda with the flour. Add to the batter and mix well.
4 With clean beaters in a clean bowl, whip the egg whites to soft peaks. Fold into the batter.
5 Pour into the prepared pan and bake 20 to 25 minutes, until a tester inserted in the center of the cake comes out clean.
6 Let the cake cool slightly in the pan on a cooling rack. Turn the cake out onto the rack and let cool completely. Remove the cake to a serving platter.
7 Make the frosting: Combine the water and brown sugar in a large saucepan on low heat. Stir until the sugar is dissolved. Add the butter. When the butter is melted, add the chocolate. Raise the heat to medium and boil for 6 minutes.
8 Remove from the heat and add the vanilla and salt. Whisk in the powdered sugar ½ cup at a time, until the frosting thickens. This may happen before all of the powdered sugar is added.
9 Spread the frosting over the cake. Allow the frosting to set, about 20 minutes.

DRUNK AND TOASTY
MYERS PECAN PIE

Babbie Myers was my stepmother Caroline's mother. She always made pecan pie for Christmas dinner, and Caroline has carried on that tradition. I added the rum—imagine that!—and made sure to use Myers's brand in honor of Babbie. This pie is based on a recipe from *Charleston Receipts*, a classic cookbook compiled and published by the Junior League of Charleston in 1950 replete with the lovely family names of the Charleston contributors, such as Manigault, Porcher, and Ravenel. A whole section is devoted to canapés, and there are recipes for such delights as syllabub, cooter pie, Huguenot torte, and hobotee. Many *Charleston Receipts* recipes cannot be improved upon, including its red rice, whose execution my Aunt Gail has absolutely perfected. I highly recommend adding *Charleston Receipts* to your cookbook collection for classic Lowcountry favorites and for inspiration.

This particular recipe has made the full evolution from the cookbook to Babbie to Caroline and to me with the addition of the Myers's rum and the step of toasting the pecans in butter and salt—a perfect salty-sweet pie your family will beg you to bring to every Thanksgiving dinner (and Christmas and Easter, too!).

Makes 1 (9-inch) pie

1 recipe Mama's Butter Piecrust (page 147)
1 cup pecan halves
2 tablespoons butter, melted
½ teaspoon kosher salt
1 cup sugar

1 cup dark corn syrup
1 tablespoon dark rum
1 teaspoon pure vanilla extract
3 large eggs, lightly beaten
Optional: 1 (6-ounce) package chocolate chips

Serving suggestion (optional): Whipped Cream (page 26) or ice cream

1 Fit the dough into a 9-inch pie dish. Trim and crimp the edges. Prebake according to the instructions. Remove to a cooling rack and reduce the oven temperature to 350°F.
2 Combine the pecans with 1 tablespoon of the melted butter and the salt and spread in a baking pan. Toast for 8 to 10 minutes, until fragrant. Set aside to cool.

3 Mix the sugar, corn syrup, the remaining 1 tablespoon butter, the rum, and vanilla. Stir in the eggs. Add the pecans and the chocolate chips, if using. Pour into the cooled piecrust.
4 Place on a rack in the lower third of the oven. Bake 50 to 60 minutes, until the center feels like Jell-O when pressed.
5 Remove to a cooling rack.

6 Serve with whipped cream or ice cream, if you wish.

Note: Proper oven temperature is particularly necessary for this recipe, so if in doubt, be sure to use an oven thermometer.

I love those weeks between Thanksgiving and Christmas. I just want to get in the kitchen and make things for people. My brother Kinnon and I were in the kitchen with the girls one day and came up with this recipe. The girls helped layer the apples and mix and sprinkle the crumb topping with their hands. Between the warm kitchen, the smell of the cinnamon-sugar apples baking, and the time spent together with Kinnon and the girls, well, even the mention of this recipe gives me the holiday spirit. You can also make this without the cast-iron skillet, rolling out the dough as for a galette (a free-form tart). It's that easy to make a special day in the kitchen, a holiday worth celebrating on its own.

Makes 1 (10-inch) tart

CHRISTMAS
CAST-IRON APPLE

6 tablespoons (¾ stick) butter
1 recipe Mama's Butter Piecrust
   (page 147)
2 pounds apples

1 tablespoon plus 1 teaspoon
   light brown sugar
1 tablespoon plus 1 teaspoon
   white sugar

1 teaspoon ground cinnamon
1 teaspoon pure vanilla extract
½ cup all-purpose flour

1 Preheat the oven to 350°F.
2 Melt 1 tablespoon of the butter in a 10-inch cast-iron skillet. Set aside to cool.
3 Roll out the piecrust into a 13-inch round and place in the skillet. You can also make a free-form tart on a baking sheet.
4 Peel, core, and thinly slice the apples. Toss with 1 tablespoon each brown and white sugar, the cinnamon, and vanilla. Lay the apples on the crust, leaving enough space around the edges to fold the dough up and over the apples by ½ to 1 inch.

5 Prepare the crumb topping by combining the flour, the remaining 1 teaspoon of each sugar, and 4 tablespoons of the butter until the mixture comes together in pea-size crumbs. Sprinkle over the apples. Fold the dough up and over the apples for a rustic look, pleating it as necessary.
6 Melt the remaining 1 tablespoon butter and brush over the exposed dough. Bake 45 minutes, or until the apples, crumb topping, and pastry are browned. Serve warm with ice cream or at room temperature.

Note: For a thicker crumb topping, combine ½ cup all-purpose flour, 2 tablespoons light brown sugar, 2 tablespoons white sugar, and 4 tablespoons butter until the mixture comes together in pea-size crumbs.

My California in-laws don't often indulge in Southern food. They say that it's too heavy, and I can understand that (to some degree!). In fact, trying to lighten up some of my Southern favorites has led to some of my best recipes. Little by little, with slight modifications to the traditional ingredients and methods, I am winning them over. This recipe is a great example of everything in moderation—it uses lighter Italian cheeses, olive oil, and half the mayonnaise of the typical recipe. Do be sure to drain the tomatoes with a sprinkling of salt for at least 30 minutes so the pie is firm rather than liquidy. And it is imperative that you peel the tomatoes.

Makes 1 (9-inch) pie

2 recipes Mama's Butter Piecrust (page 147)
6 large tomatoes (2 pounds)
¼ teaspoon kosher salt
½ cup mayonnaise

6 tablespoons olive oil
1 cup grated Parmesan cheese
⅓ cup grated Pecorino Romano cheese
Freshly ground black pepper

4 green onions, minced (white and green parts)
15 fresh basil leaves, torn into small pieces

1 Roll out and fit half the dough into a 9-inch pie dish. Trim the edges. Prebake at 400°F according to the instructions. Remove to a cooling rack and reduce the oven temperature to 350°F.
2 While the crust bakes, peel and core the tomatoes (see page 157). Slice or chop the tomatoes and sprinkle with the salt. Drain in a colander for at least 30 minutes.

3 Combine the mayonnaise, olive oil, Parmesan, and Romano.
4 When the bottom piecrust has cooled, spread one-third of the mayonnaise mixture evenly in the bottom of the crust. Scatter one-third of the tomatoes in a layer and sprinkle with pepper, one-third of the green onions, and then one-third of the basil. Repeat the layers 2 more times, starting with the mayonnaise mixture and finishing with the basil, or until all the ingredients are used.

5 Roll out the other crust and place on top. Crimp the bottom and top crusts together. Use the tip of a knife to make a few slits for steam to escape.
6 Bake 35 to 45 minutes, until the top is golden. Let cool slightly before cutting.

Note: Serve with a salad for a light meal or with meat and a vegetable for a hearty supper.

LIGHTER LOWCOUNTRY TOMATO PIE

Peeling Tomatoes and Peaches

I don't typically peel my peaches, but if you do, there's a good method for peeling tomatoes that works well on peaches, too. I usually peel my tomatoes by hand with a knife, but when I need to peel several tomatoes, I parboil them. Bring a pot of water to a boil. Insert a fork in the stem end of the tomato or peach. Use a paring knife to cut an X in the opposite end. Place in the boiling water for 15 seconds. The X cut will lift up the skin and you can peel the tomato or peach with four easy pulls.

Vidalias are the stars of this savory treat. If you have some on hand and a piecrust in the freezer, you can pull together this simple showstopper in a snap. You can even leave out the bacon if you want to make it vegetarian—the onions are that flavor-ful. I really like sweet pies, but I *love* a savory pie and this rustic version is hands-down one of my favorites.

Makes 1 (9- to 10-inch) rustic tart

CARAMELIZED VIDALIA ONION GALETTE

1 recipe Mama's Butter Piecrust (page 147)
4 tablespoons (½ stick) butter
3 pounds Vidalia onions (or other sweet variety such as Walla-Walla and Texas 1015), cut in half and thinly sliced

1 teaspoon minced garlic
Kosher salt
¼ teaspoon freshly ground black pepper
1½ tablespoons Dijon mustard

Optional: 1½ teaspoons fresh thyme leaves
1 cup grated Parmesan cheese
1 egg, beaten
Optional: 4 slices bacon, cooked, drained, and chopped

1 Preheat the oven to 400°F.
2 Roll out the dough to a 12-inch circle. Place the dough on a baking sheet lined with parchment paper.
3 Melt the butter in a large skillet on low heat. Add the onions and stir to coat with the butter. After 5 minutes, add the garlic. Continue to cook the onions, stirring occasionally. In 20 minutes, the onions will soften and shrink in the pan. In 30 to 40 minutes, they will be golden brown.
4 Season with salt to taste and the pepper. Stir in the mustard and the thyme, if using.
5 Sprinkle the crust with ⅓ cup of the Parmesan. Pile the onions in the center and spread to within 2 inches of the edge. Fold the dough up to and over the onions, pleating it as necessary. Brush the crust with the egg.
6 Place in the oven. Check after 10 to 15 minutes. When the crust begins to color, sprinkle the top with the remaining ⅔ cup Parmesan and the bacon, if using. Bake 10 to 15 minutes more. Put the oven rack in the top position. Turn on the broiler and broil 3 to 5 minutes, until deeply brown. Watch carefully, as ovens vary in broiling intensity.

159

A CUP A CUP A COBBLER

When I need a dessert to take somewhere, there is nothing simpler nor more universally loved by all than this cobbler. It really is as easy as a cup of this and a cup of that. And it's incredibly versatile—you can experiment with different fruits and berries. You'll figure out which fruit or combination of fruits is your favorite, but I promise you they'll all taste good, especially served warm from the oven with a little ice cream on top.

Makes 1 (9-inch) cobbler

8 tablespoons (1 stick) butter
1 cup white sugar
1 cup self-rising flour
2 tablespoons light brown sugar

⅛ teaspoon ground cinnamon
1 cup whole milk
1 teaspoon pure vanilla extract

2 cups berries and/or diced peaches (if frozen, do not thaw)
1 lemon wedge

1 Preheat the oven to 350°F.
2 Melt the butter and pour into a 9-inch pie dish.
3 Combine the white sugar, flour, 1 tablespoon of the brown sugar, the cinnamon, milk, and vanilla in a bowl. Whisk just to combine. The batter will be lumpy. Pour the batter into the pie dish. Pour the fruit over the batter and give the dish a shake to even out the distribution.
4 Bake for 45 to 60 minutes, until golden brown.
5 Remove from the oven and sprinkle with the remaining 1 tablespoon brown sugar. Let cool. Spritz with the lemon just before serving.

WAFFLE WAFFLE
WAFFLES

I almost wish I could give these waffles their own chapter—and not just because they taste so delicious. When I was a little girl, I lived with my dad. Some nights he would have to work late. But no matter how late it was, he would come into my room and whisper in my ear, "Waffle waffle waffle!" I'd wake up and we'd go to the kitchen, where he'd make waffles. It was an absolutely magical time for me—in the kitchen with my dad in what felt like the middle of the night eating waffles and talking about our day.

Dad is a no-frills cook. His waffle recipe was to mix together pancake mix from the box with a can of creamed corn. But from that simple recipe came one of the most important memories of my life. He gave me a magical childhood and showed me that I was always on his mind, always his priority, always special.

He was and is an incredible parent. I'm always trying to emulate him, but even though I have all the support and guidance in the world, I'm still working at being as good a parent as he is. He taught me that the two most important things about parenting are unconditional love and teaching children to be independent and responsible for their actions. He taught me to look people in the face, and when I was a child, he demanded I shake adults' hands and introduce myself. He taught me confidence and taught me to position myself as an expert no matter what my chosen field. He taught me "red on right on return" for navigating waterways in the boat. How to throw a cast net and how to clean a crab. Everything I know about life I learned from him.

He is my hero. I am so grateful to him for all he has taught me, all he has sacrificed for me, and all the support and love he continues to give me. I have dressed up Dad's waffle "recipe," but nothing can top the magic of his voice in my ear in the middle of the night: "Waffle waffle waffle!"

Makes 4 to 6 Belgian-style waffles

2 cups all-purpose flour
1 tablespoon baking soda
1 tablespoon sugar
½ teaspoon ground cinnamon
2 large eggs

1½ cups creamed corn (a little less than one 14.75-ounce can)
1½ cups buttermilk
12 tablespoons (1½ sticks) butter, melted

½ teaspoon pure vanilla extract
Serving suggestion: Warm maple syrup

1 Follow the manufacturer's directions for greasing and preheating the waffle iron. If you want to hold the waffles, preheat the oven to 200°F and put a cooling rack placed over a baking sheet in the oven. (Putting the waffles in the warm oven makes them nice and crispy—just the way I like them!)

2 Combine the flour, baking soda, sugar, and cinnamon in a large bowl and whisk to blend.
3 Lightly beat the eggs in another bowl. Add the corn and buttermilk and blend well. Stir in the butter and vanilla. Pour into the flour mixture and mix well.
4 Cook the waffles according to the waffle maker directions.

5 Serve the waffles immediately as you make them, or keep warm in the oven to serve all at once. Serve with warm maple syrup.

Variation: Add 1 cup chopped cooked bacon and 1 cup shredded sharp cheddar cheese to the batter and garnish with chopped green onions or chives.

I'm not a big breakfast person. I'd rather save my calories for lunch and supper. So John is in charge of big weekend breakfasts, and this recipe was one his mother made for him and that he now makes for the girls. Every time they have a friend spend the night, they request that John make a puffy pancake. They drag their little chairs from the playroom to the kitchen and sit in front of the oven waiting so they can watch and squeal with delight when the pancake puffs up. Then they get to sprinkle powdered sugar on top before finally getting to enjoy the yummy taste of the Saturday morning puffy pancake show.

Makes 2 to 4 servings

JOHN'S PUFFY PANCAKE

3 large eggs
½ cup whole milk
2 tablespoons fresh orange juice
½ teaspoon pure vanilla extract
½ teaspoon ground cinnamon
½ teaspoon grated lemon zest

½ cup plus 2 tablespoons cake flour or all-purpose flour, sifted
4 tablespoons (½ stick) butter

GARNISHES
Fresh lemon juice and powdered sugar

Sautéed apples and whipped cream
Roasted pears
Fresh berries with lemon juice or a honey drizzle
Bananas and whipped cream with brown sugar, cinnamon, and white sugar

1 Preheat the oven to 450°F.
2 Combine the eggs, milk, and juice. Mix well. Add the vanilla, cinnamon, and lemon zest. Gently add the flour. Mix well with a whisk.

3 Melt the butter in a 10- to 12-inch cast-iron skillet on medium heat. Pour in the batter. Cook 60 to 90 seconds to set the batter. Place the skillet in the oven.
4 Bake 20 to 25 minutes, until the pancake has puffed, the sides are crisp and brown, and the center is golden.
5 Serve immediately with the garnish of your choice.

MS. EM'S BREAD

My Aunt Emily (that's right, Auntie Em!) spent the first fifteen years of her marriage on a remote farm in what we called the "wilderness" of Colorado. She had plenty of time to experiment in the kitchen and became an incredible self-taught cook and baker. I imagine her as a young wife, the winds of the Rockies howling outside her door, her warm kitchen full of the comforting smell of baking bread. This recipe has been passed through the family, as it is easy and delicious. I make multiple batches for Christmas presents that tend to garner multiple requests for the recipe. Similar to a French loaf in style, it's perfect as a side for hearty cool-weather favorites such as stews and pot roasts.

Makes 1 loaf

- 1 (¼-ounce) package active dry yeast
- ¼ cup warm water
- 3 cups all-purpose flour
- 1 teaspoon kosher salt, plus more for sprinkling on top
- 1 teaspoon sugar
- 1½ cups cold water
- 2 teaspoons olive oil
- Optional toppings: ½ teaspoon cracked black pepper, 1 tablespoon sesame seeds

1 Preheat the oven to 425°F.
2 Dissolve the yeast in the warm water and set aside.
3 Mix the flour, the 1 teaspoon salt, and sugar in a large bowl. Add the dissolved yeast and mix well. Stir in the cold water little by little. The dough will be wet. Cover the dough with a damp kitchen towel and let sit for 45 minutes to rise.
4 Coat the inside of an 8-inch loaf pan with ½ to 1 teaspoon of the olive oil. Pour the dough into the pan without kneading or punching it down. It will be almost liquid in consistency. Brush the top with the remaining olive oil and sprinkle with about ¼ teaspoon salt and the optional toppings if you wish.
5 Bake for 25 to 30 minutes, until the top is golden brown and the sides pull away from the pan. Wait to cool before cutting. This bread freezes well.

When Sean Brock opened up his now famous restaurant Husk in Charleston, one of the first desserts on his menu was an oatmeal cream pie. His opening happened to be close to my daughter Cate's birthday. Inspired, I decided to make and send oatmeal cream pies to her class for her birthday instead of cupcakes. Just the idea of "cream filling" is thrilling for children—and for anyone who ever was a child. For the birthday pies, I wrapped each one in parchment paper, then gathered the paper on top and tied it with a pretty ribbon. The pies were a huge, yummy, gooey hit in Cate's classroom.

You can roll the cream sides in sprinkles or chocolate chips. This is another recipe that's fun to experiment with and create variations using different kinds of cookies and garnishes for the cream filling. You can also use store-bought cookies, or refrigerated-dough cookies. A stand mixer is good for this recipe.

Makes 4 dozen cookies, 3 cups filling (enough for 2 to 4 dozen sandwich cookies)

OATMEAL CREAM PIES

OATMEAL-RAISIN COOKIES
10 tablespoons (1¼ sticks) butter
¾ cup firmly packed light brown sugar
½ cup white sugar
2 large eggs, at room temperature
1 teaspoon pure vanilla extract
1½ cups all-purpose flour
1 teaspoon baking soda
1 teaspoon ground cinnamon
½ teaspoon kosher salt
3 cups uncooked rolled oats (quick or old-fashioned)
1 cup raisins
1 cup chocolate chips

CREAM PIE FILLING
2 cups powdered sugar, sifted
½ pound (2 sticks) butter, at room temperature
1 (16-ounce) container marshmallow creme
1 teaspoon pure vanilla extract
½ teaspoon ground cinnamon
Pinch of kosher salt
Garnish (optional): Colored sprinkles or mini chocolate chips

1 Make the cookies: Preheat the oven to 350°F.
2 Beat the butter, brown sugar, and white sugar together with an electric mixer until creamy, 6 to 8 minutes. Mix in the eggs and vanilla.
3 Whisk the flour, baking soda, cinnamon, and salt together in a separate bowl. Add to the butter mixture and mix well. Add the oats. Mix well. (If your mixer is not very powerful, you may have to do this mixing by hand.) Fold in the raisins and chocolate chips.
4 Drop by the tablespoon on ungreased baking sheets, ½ inch apart. Bake 8 to 10 minutes, until the cookies are light golden brown.
5 Let cool briefly on the pans, then remove to racks to cool completely. If baking multiple batches on the same baking sheet, make sure the baking sheet cools before you put the dough on it.

6 Make the filling: Beat the sugar, butter, and marshmallow creme with an electric mixer until well blended. Mix in the vanilla, cinnamon, and salt.
7 Make the pies: Spoon the filling onto the flat side of half the cookies. Top each with another cookie and squeeze gently. Roll the edges in sprinkles or chocolate chips, if you'd like. Store in an airtight container.

MAXCEY'S THIN AND CRISPY CHOCOLATE CHIP COOKIES

Great-grandmother Maxcey was Mama's mother. These are her delicious, small, crispy cookies. I perfected these during a chocolate chip cookie bake-off with my brother Miles, who's been making cookies for as long as he could reach the store-bought break-and-bake cookie dough in the refrigerator. Miles brought in the big guns for our little competition, a recipe from Thomas Keller's cookbook *Ad Hoc at Home*. I combined Great-Grandmother Maxcey's recipe with a technique from Grandmama from the other side of my family: Once the dough is on the baking sheet but before you bake it, you hold the sheet 2 feet or so above the kitchen counter and then drop it. The impact of the sheet hitting the counter spreads the dough, making the cookies super thin. Miles delivered perfect big and chewy chocolate chip cookies, but I think even Miles would agree that the cookies I made were some of the most fabulous cookies we'd ever tasted. And if that's not fabulous enough for you, take these cookies to the next level by making ice cream sandwiches with them. Yum.

Makes 130 to 140 small cookies

8 tablespoons (1 stick) butter, plus more for the baking sheets
½ cup vegetable shortening
1 cup white sugar
¾ cup packed light brown sugar
1 teaspoon pure vanilla extract
2 large eggs, at room temperature, lightly beaten
1 tablespoon baking soda
1 tablespoon hot water
2¼ cups sifted all-purpose flour
1 teaspoon kosher salt
1 cup chopped pecans
2 (12-ounce) packages chocolate chips

1 Preheat the oven to 350°F. Line 2 or more baking sheets with parchment paper and coat lightly with butter.

2 Cream the 8 tablespoons butter and the shortening with an electric mixer on medium speed for about 2 minutes, or until fluffy. Add the white and brown sugars and the vanilla and beat 6 to 8 minutes, until well incorporated. Beat in the eggs.

3 Dissolve the baking soda in the hot water and mix in. Sift the flour and salt together and mix in. (You might have to do this by hand.) Fold in the pecans and chocolate chips.

4 Drop by the ½ teaspoon about ½ inch apart onto the buttered, parchment-lined baking sheets. Lift each baking sheet with cookie dough and drop to the counter before baking.

5 Bake 8 to 10 minutes, until the cookies are brown and their surface appears dull rather than shiny. Let cool briefly on the pans, then remove to racks to cool completely. If baking multiple batches on the same baking sheet, make sure the baking sheet cools before you put the dough on it.

PECAN SANDS

Grandmama always made these cookies at Christmastime. I can picture her home in Gaffney and these cookies on her dessert table. During my teenage and college years, my mother hosted a Christmas Eve party and Grandmama would come, bringing her pecan sands with her. All of my friends knew my mother's house was the place to go on Christmas Eve once their own family obligations were done—my mother, stepfather, Grandmama, and I would stay up late keeping the party going, putting together toys for my little brothers, and enjoying the party food leftovers including duck and sausage gumbo, country ham biscuits with Grandmama's relish, strawberries dipped in toasted pecan mousse, and pecan sands. You might even say the real party started once the invited guests had already left! These cookies remind me of the good times (and good food) my grandmother always brought to the party and that my mother continues to bring. I hope that's a family tradition I carry on as well—I'm at least giving it a darn good try!

Makes 80 cookies

3 cups all-purpose flour
⅓ cup white sugar
½ pound (2 sticks) cold butter, cut in cubes

4 teaspoons pure vanilla extract
1 cup finely chopped pecans
Optional: 1 tablespoon ice water

Powdered sugar, sifted

1 Preheat the oven to 350°F. Line baking sheets with parchment paper.
2 Combine the flour and white sugar in a large bowl. Add the butter and use your hands to mix together. Work in the vanilla and the pecans, adding ice water if needed for the dough to come together.
3 Shape the dough into balls, using 1 teaspoon batter for one-bite cookies or 1 tablespoon batter for two-bite cookies. Place on the baking sheet ½ inch apart.
4 Bake for 10 to 12 minutes. The dough will not brown.
5 Transfer the cookies, still on the parchment paper, to a cooling rack. When cool enough to handle, roll the cookies in sifted powdered sugar. If baking multiple batches on the same baking sheet, make sure the baking sheet cools before you put the dough on it. Store the sands in an airtight container.

ENTERTAINING

I like to enjoy myself when I entertain, so I find it does help to be organized. And I don't need everything to be perfect or even seem perfect, because I'm not perfect! As much as I do enjoy putting together a little atmosphere and décor, for me it's all about the food. Does it taste good? Is everyone raving about it? Does everyone leave with a full belly and the taste of good drinks on their lips?

My best dishes and drinks are not complicated. The secret to their goodness is using the best and freshest ingredients and not taking shortcuts. Using fresh herbs, chopping fresh vegetables, brining the turkey—these are the extra but simple steps that really elevate the food. To take that extra step with every dish and every aspect of entertaining is daunting. That's why I pick the dishes I want to do, give them my best effort, and purchase or delegate the rest. I love introducing my guests to local products made by local people committed to creating good food and drink, so it really is a win-win situation of helping a local business and giving myself a break.

For each of the occasions featured in this chapter, I've included some of my favorite recipes. But what I hope you'll find is that most of the recipes in this book are pretty versatile and that there are plenty that are equally appropriate for an oyster roast, a family meal around the kitchen table, or a cocktail party! So I've listed other recipes from the book you may also want to consider for each occasion, and hopefully you'll come up with even more good ideas I haven't even thought about yet.

No matter the occasion, whether it's a sit-down holiday dinner or a picnic in the backyard, start with making the best-tasting food you can and the rest will come. And you'll never have a shortage of friends who are just as delighted by your boiled peanuts as your Champagne cocktails.

Sit-Down Holiday Dinner

THANKSGIVING MENU

Sage Butter-Roasted Turkey (page 181)

Grandmama's Classic Squash Casserole (page 182)

Cast-Iron Green Beans with Soy and Sesame (page 69)

Dressing (not "stuffing"—people in the South don't stuff their turkeys)

Rice and gravy

Biscuits (pages 17 and 22)

Fresh cranberry sauce

Drunk and Toasty Myers Pecan Pie (page 152)

CHRISTMAS MENU

Standing Rib Roast (page 184)

Potato Gratin (page 187)

Haricots verts or roasted asparagus (see page 65)

Grapefruit and avocado salad

French rolls

Chocolate dessert

ADDITIONAL OR ALTERNATE RECIPES

Black Pepper Biscuits (page 20)

Caroline's Macaroni Pie (page 70)

Roasted vegetables (see page 65)

Vegetable Gratin (page 61)

Alex's Chocolate Chess Pie (page 150)

Sweet Tea with Mint (page 242)

I want to host Thanksgiving and Christmas dinner every year. I don't want to eat at someone else's house. (Except maybe my mother's—she's my inspiration for this kind of entertaining.) I love to do it, and I want to do it, and my family lets me do it most of the time. My entertaining style is relatively informal and even simple. But that doesn't mean I'm not a control freak about it! Especially for these holiday meals. The menu is everything to me, and I make the same thing every year: the family dishes that have been passed down and embody the holidays for me. It really isn't Thanksgiving without Grandmama's squash casserole. And if I have to go somewhere else for the meal, I'm either taking it with me or fixing it for myself to have at home later that day.

Along those lines, since I want to keep the menu intact, when guests ask me what they can bring, I am very specific. And people seem to appreciate the direction most of the time. You don't want a bunch of different sides or casseroles—what my friends and family know I like to call "the riff-raff"—that may or may not go with the rest of the food. So be specific with whatever food item you'd like them to bring, or ask that they bring wine or Champagne.

My friends and family know how much I love to throw spontaneous get-togethers, but for the holidays I not only like to plan ahead, I like to take my time and enjoy each step of the process. Below is the schedule I usually follow and some décor I like to include. Use it as inspiration and then make it your own! You'll notice I like to use things I already have or can easily and inexpensively collect or create. Using recipes, serving pieces, and décor I've used time and time again is part of my holiday tradition. As I order the turkey, pull out the linen tablecloth, the holiday spirit just rises up inside me. I look forward to every element of the preparations, and then I savor the day itself with family, friends, and good, good, good food.

A WEEK OR TWO AHEAD OF DINNER

- Finalize the guest list.
- Order the turkey or standing rib roast. Plan for 1 pound of meat per four to six people. When ordering a standing rib roast, be sure to ask the butcher to trim the roast.
- Order rolls. I get mine from Normandy Farms Bakery. If no one is bringing a dessert, I order the dessert as well.
- Delegate tasks to those who ask to bring something. Here's what I usually ask people to bring:

Champagne and wine

Dessert My stepmother, Caroline, always brings pecan pie for Thanksgiving, and I usually ask someone to bring something chocolaty for Christmas.

Charcuterie for an appetizer during the cocktail hour—I even tell them where to get it, if they ask!

- Make a shopping list.
- Pull out your special serving pieces and any cherished holiday items from cabinets or storage. I like to turn on some music and put cinnamon sticks, orange peel, and star anise in water to simmer on the stove so the whole house smells like Christmas while

I take my time getting out those pieces I tend to use only during the holidays. Rediscovering them after not seeing them for a year is like receiving them as a gift all over again or revisiting the happy memories I associate with each one. Enjoy the moment!

THE WEEK OF THE DINNER

• Do the grocery shopping.

• Begin the turkey preparations, but do not worry about the number of steps involved. None of the steps is complicated and you can break them down and accomplish them over a few days. Make the turkey brine and brine the turkey 1 to 3 days ahead. You can also prepare the turkey up to the point of roasting.

• Rub down the standing rib roast 1 to 3 days ahead. Your refrigerator will smell divine.

• Make the squash casserole the day before so that it's ready to be baked the day of.

• Prepare biscuits the day before if you're serving biscuits. Also go ahead and put out whatever serving piece you plan on using to serve your biscuits. I have some rustic wooden bowls I like to use. I line the bowls with linen napkins a day or so ahead of time just to have that out of the way. Then the day of the dinner, when I pull the hot reheated biscuits from the oven, I wrap them in the linen napkin inside the bowl and put the bowl on the dining room table for people to help themselves.

• Wrap up rolls for heating the day before if you're having them, so that the day-of they are ready to be put in the oven. I serve rolls just like I do the biscuits—wrapped in a linen napkin in a rustic wooden bowl. I really like that juxtaposition of simple wood container and elegant napkin—another example of my entertaining style being a reflection of my personality! A little bit plain and a little bit fancy.

• Plan seating arrangements, including making sure there is a place for everyone. One year we had so many people coming that my dad had to make a hinged piece of plywood to put on top of my dining room table to make a bigger surface.

• Make place cards. This is a fun activity for my girls—especially when it involves them gathering up the raw materials themselves outside in the yard.

Morey Girls' Favorite Place Cards/Place Card Holders

Pinecones with cards held between the scales.
Fall leaves with names written in metallic pen.
Christmas ornaments with cards attached to the top.

• Make the centerpieces. As I've said, for me it's all about the food, so I keep the décor simple. Be sure your centerpiece is not so tall that people sitting across the table have a hard time seeing one another or conversing.

Holiday Centerpieces

Short, tight flower arrangements in containers you already own. I like to use mint julep cups, water glasses, or mason jars with votive candles interspersed among the arrangements. You can use flowers from the yard, leaves from the yard, fallen leaves off the ground, or fresh herbs. As always, the gathering is part of the fun!

Holly leaves and berries or magnolia leaves gathered from the yard placed around votives.

Fresh Christmas garland laid out flat on the table with votives. You can also add holly leaves, berries, and magnolia leaves into the greenery.

Interesting-looking fresh vegetables in bowls or baskets.

Clove oranges in a bowl. My girls love doing this! Pierce orange skins with a toothpick either randomly or in a pattern. Insert whole cloves into the holes. Looks elegant and smells amazing.

Sugared fruit in a bowl. the girls love this one, too. Dip pieces of fruit (I like to use cherries, grapes, strawberries, lemons, and limes) in egg whites and then in white sugar. Let dry on a cooling rack.

• Prepare the linens. This is a case of doing as I say rather than as I do. I collect old linens, and I absolutely love them, but for some reason, ironing them is something I always leave to the last minute. Linen irons so easily and it takes only a second per napkin or hand towel, and yet my friends will tell you they have walked into my house just as the party is starting and I'm ironing napkins on the bed in the guest room! So make sure your tablecloths, napkins, and hand towels for the bathroom and bar are clean and ironed ahead of time. Sometimes, as when we had the handy plywood extension on the table, more than one tablecloth is required, and I layer different tablecloths for a shabby chic look. It's pretty special to have my tablecloth on the table along with my Aunt Gail's seventy-year-old tablecloth that she let me borrow. If something is a family heirloom and you love it, it somehow always looks and feels just right whether it matches perfectly or not.

• Set the table. I like to wrap the napkins in twine with a sprig of rosemary or a cinnamon stick. (You can do this same thing for a different party, with basil or cilantro.) Make an event out of this step by involving children, family, or friends and serving mocktails/cocktails and snacks. My stepmother, Caroline, always helps me polish the silver, and my Aunt Gail comes early the day of the dinner, and we drink Bloody Marys and set the table—but this can certainly be done earlier than the day of.

• Set up the children's table. I set up a separate table for the children, covered in white craft paper. The girls and I draw a placemat at each child's place right on the paper with crayon, with his or her name on it. Then we make a centerpiece of crayons in glasses or mason jars so the children can continue to decorate the "tablecloth" themselves during the meal while the adults take their time eating and talking.

• Find a place for your personal touch or special pieces. I collect old linens. Whenever I go on a trip, I like to check out flea markets or antique shops and get cocktail napkins, dinner napkins, or hand towels. I can sometimes even find a C or an M monogrammed on them. I love mixing and matching them. Not only do I use dinner napkins at the table, but I also use cocktail napkins at the bar, a nice hand towel at the bar, and a nice hand towel in the bathroom. I also collect silver mint julep cups. You can find these new or as antiques in sterling or in silver plate, and they can be used not only for drinks, but also for flower arrangements, to put utensils in, to put cut celery in for Bloody Marys. The options are endless, and the presentation really is elegant. Candlelight shimmers off of them beautifully. And finally, one reason I can't wait to host the holiday dinners is that I get to use Grandmama's silver gravy boat. I always loved it growing up, and I begged for it for years. Then when I hosted my first Christmas dinner as a married woman, Grandmama gave it to me as a Christmas gift. I cherish it! Not as much as I cherish her squash casserole recipe, but almost. Even if you do not have a family heirloom passed down to you, you can start your own family heirloom with a linen collection, a collection of antique silver spoons, an unusual carving set or cake plate—whatever you love and whatever will make you smile every holiday season when you pull it out for your dinner table.

THE DAY OF THE DINNER

- Bake the squash, dressing, and/or gratin before the guests arrive and cover in foil to keep warm.
- Prepare the ham biscuits for the cocktail hour.
- Have the rice staying warm on the stove in the rice steamer.
- Time the cooking of the turkey or roast so that it finishes up during cocktail hour.
- While the turkey or roast rests before carving, make the gravy, cook the green beans, asparagus, or haricots verts, and heat the rolls or bake the biscuits in the oven.
- If serving the turkey or roast from a tray, you can put washed magnolia leaves or raw collard greens under the tray or even on the tray under the meat for an extra garnish.
- Even if it's not all that cold, make a fire in the fireplace. If it's a warm Lowcountry holiday, I just turn down the air conditioner temp a little bit more. That's how much I love a fire. It creates the perfect atmosphere for a holiday party and gives off a stunning light you could never re-create. Why have a fireplace if you don't use it? Even if it is 70 degrees outside . . .
- When everyone arrives, make sure they get a drink and a bite to whet the conversation and the palate. I like Champagne cocktails and Bloody Marys for holiday occasions, but I set up a full bar so people can help themselves and make what they'd like. (See page 191 for more about setting up a good bar.) For the children, I make mocktails in fancy glasses with flavored soda, a splash of freshly squeezed juice, a slice of fruit on the rim for garnish, and a pretty straw. For cocktail hour bites, there's the charcuterie a thoughtful guest has brought, and, of course, no cocktail hour passes through my house without buttermilk biscuits stuffed with finely chopped country ham. Ham biscuits and a glass of Champagne make the perfect marriage, and this happy pairing sets just the right tone to begin the party.
- Let everyone serve themselves. I set up the buffet of food in my kitchen. I put gravy, rolls, and biscuits on the dining table.
- Keep the flow moving. Whether this means making sure everyone has what they need, or that everyone is able to sit down to eat at the time you see fit, or trying to keep the tone positive when family tensions arise, do your best to keep the party afloat and your guests feeling at ease. Embrace the "lively" conversation and diverse personalities of your loved ones (this is easier said than done at times!), and—most important—keep the food and drinks a'comin'.

SAGE BUTTER-ROASTED TURKEY

Do not be daunted by the number of steps! The process is not too complicated, and the preparation can be divided so you can spread it out over a few days.

Makes 10 to 12 servings

BRINE AND TURKEY
1½ cups kosher salt
½ cup sugar
1 tablespoon whole black peppercorns
2 lemons, sliced
2 cups water
2 gallons ice water

Juice of 1 lemon
1 (12- to 15-pound) fresh turkey

4 tablespoons (½ stick) butter, cut in 8 slices
8 fresh sage leaves
2 tablespoons olive oil
3 carrots, cut in chunks

3 stalks celery, cut in chunks
2 onions, quartered
Freshly ground black pepper
Optional, for pan gravy: about 2 tablespoons all-purpose flour and 1 cup or more unsalted chicken or turkey stock

1 Brine the turkey: In a stockpot large enough to hold the turkey, combine the salt, sugar, peppercorns, lemons, and 2 cups water. Bring to a boil and stir to dissolve the salt and sugar. Remove from the heat and add the ice water and lemon juice. Submerge the turkey, cover, and refrigerate 6 to 8 hours or overnight.
2 Remove the turkey from the brine and rinse under cold running water. Place on a cooling rack to drain and dry the skin with a clean kitchen towel (or paper towels).
3 Prepare a sheet of aluminum foil to cover the breast of the turkey if it begins to brown too quickly. Cut and mold the foil when the turkey is cold so you can easily slip the foil over the breast, if needed. Set aside this "tent."
4 Using your fingers, gently separate the skin of the legs, thighs, and breast from the flesh. Poke the pieces of butter and the sage leaves under the skin. Dry the bird again and rub with the oil. Prepare a nest in a shallow roasting pan with the carrots, celery, and onions and place the turkey on the nest. Sprinkle with pepper. Refrigerate uncovered. (This can be done the night before.)
5 Two hours before cooking, remove the turkey from the fridge. Preheat the oven to 450°F.
6 If any liquid has collected in the roasting pan, remove it with a turkey baster. Tuck the wings under the turkey and tie the legs together with kitchen twine.

7 Place the turkey in the oven with the legs facing the rear. Lower the temperature to 350°F. Rotate the turkey back-to-front after 1 hour. Baste, if desired, every 30 minutes.
8 Roast 2 hours 30 minutes to 2 hours 45 minutes, until a digital thermometer inserted into the thigh registers 170°F.
9 Remove the turkey to a cutting board and let rest 30 minutes before carving.
10 Reserve the drippins for gravy, if you like. (See page 80 for how to make pan gravy.) Be sure to taste the drippins as they can be salty from a brined bird—you don't want to add too much salt to the gravy if the drippins are good and salty already.

GRANDMAMA'S CLASSIC SQUASH CASSEROLE

Makes 8 servings

6 tablespoons (¾ stick) butter: 2 tablespoons melted, 4 tablespoons cut in bits
4 or 5 yellow squash (1½ to 2 pounds)
1 cup chopped yellow onion

4 large eggs
¾ teaspoon kosher salt, or more to taste
⅛ teaspoon freshly ground black pepper, or more to taste
2 cups whole milk

1 pound Monterey Jack cheese, shredded
1 cup dry breadcrumbs or crushed crackers (such as Ritz or Waverly Wafers)

1 Preheat the oven to 350°F. Brush a 2-quart casserole dish with the melted butter.
2 Slice the narrow neck of the squash into rounds. Cut the fatter bodies into quarters and chop.
3 Combine the squash and onion in a saucepan with just enough water to cover, and simmer 5 to 7 minutes, until the squash are tender. Drain well in a colander.
4 Beat the eggs in a large bowl with the salt and pepper. Stir in the milk and cheese and mix well. Add the squash and mix. Pour into the casserole dish.

Top with the breadcrumbs and dot with the remaining 4 tablespoons butter.
5 Bake 30 to 45 minutes, until the top is lightly browned and puffed.

Makes 12 to 16 servings

1 (10- to 12-pound) rib roast
1½ tablespoons kosher salt
Freshly ground black pepper
Olive oil

10 to 15 cloves garlic
3 large shallots, cut in half
Leaves from 4 sprigs fresh basil
Leaves from 4 sprigs fresh rosemary

Leaves from 4 sprigs fresh thyme
1 cup coarsely chopped carrots
1 cup sliced onion

STANDING RIB ROAST

1 Line a baking sheet with foil and top with a cooling rack. Place the roast on the rack. Season all over with the salt and pepper to taste. Rub olive oil on the ends of the bones.

2 Place the garlic and shallots in a mini food processor and pulse until chopped. Add the basil, rosemary, and thyme. With the machine running, pour in olive oil and process to a chunky consistency. Rub the herb paste over the roast. Loosely cover with plastic wrap and refrigerate 1 to 3 days.

3 At least 3 hours before you will begin cooking, remove the roast from the fridge to come to room temperature.

4 Preheat the oven to 450°F and place an oven rack in the lower third of the oven.

5 Scrape off most of the herb paste. Dry the roast with a clean kitchen towel (or paper towels). Secure the meat to the ribs by tying kitchen twine in between each rib section.

6 Prepare a nest in a shallow roasting pan with the carrots and onion and place the roast, bones down, on the nest. Put the roast in the oven with the bones facing the door.

7 Roast for 30 minutes. You should hear the fat start to melt and sizzle and there will be some browning.

8 Reduce the oven temperature to 325°F. Roast for 1 hour 30 minutes, then begin to take the temperature of the meat, checking every 10 minutes or so from this point on.

9 Remove the roast at 110°F for rare meat or at 120°F for medium-rare. (The temperature will continue to rise after the roast is removed from the oven.) Reserve the meat juices to spoon over the beef. Let the meat rest 30 minutes before carving. Tent with foil if your kitchen is chilly.

Standing Rib Roast

Order your rib roast in advance and ask the butcher to trim it for you. The cut of beef you want is called a standing rib roast, a rib roast, or sometimes prime rib.

Season your roast 1 to 3 days before cooking and store, loosely covered, in the fridge.

On the day that you plan to cook the roast, remove it from the fridge at least 3 hours before you begin cooking.

Have a digital thermometer on hand to test doneness.

Plan on letting the cooked roast rest 30 minutes before carving.

POTATO GRATIN

Makes 6 to 8 servings

4 tablespoons (½ stick) butter:
  2 tablespoons at room
  temperature, 2 tablespoons
  cut in 8 pieces
4 large cloves garlic, peeled

2 cups milk
2 cups whipping cream
1½ to 2 teaspoons kosher salt,
  plus more as needed
4 large russet (baking) potatoes
  (about 3 pounds)

Freshly ground black pepper
3 cups shredded Gruyère cheese
  (imported preferred)

1 Preheat the oven to 350°F. Butter a 2-quart casserole dish with the 2 tablespoons room-temperature butter and rub with 1 of the garlic cloves. Discard the clove.

2 Combine the milk and cream in a large saucepan. Add the salt and taste to be sure it tastes salty. Add the remaining 3 garlic cloves and bring to a boil, then reduce the heat and simmer 5 minutes, being careful not to let the mixture boil over.

3 Meanwhile, peel and rinse the potatoes. Pat dry. Using a mandoline, slicer, or knife, cut into ⅛-inch-thick slices. Making a circular pattern, overlap the slices to cover the bottom of the casserole.

4 Top with ¼ cup of the milk mixture and a few grinds of pepper, a sprinkle of salt, and ¾ cup of the cheese. Repeat this layering, reserving ½ cup of the cheese, until you have only ½ inch left at the top of the dish.

5 Use a slotted spoon to remove the garlic, and pour the remaining milk mixture through a strainer into the casserole until the potatoes are covered. You might not use all the milk. Do not overfill the casserole dish—maintain a ½ inch of space at the top of the dish once the milk sinks in. Top with the reserved cheese and scatter the butter pieces over the top.

6 Line a baking sheet with foil and place the casserole dish on the sheet. Bake 30 to 45 minutes, until the top is bubbling, the cheese is brown, and a knife easily pierces the potatoes. Let rest 10 to 12 minutes, then serve.

Cocktail Celebration

MENU

Cast-Iron Roasted Oysters (page 194)

Callie's 498 Meeting Street Crab (page 196)

Bacon–Green Onion Savory Crisps (page 198)

Tuna Tartare (page 199)

Shrimp Bruschetta (page 200)

Ham biscuits

Finger sandwiches

Savory Roasted Pecans (page 202)

ADDITIONAL OR ALTERNATE RECIPES

Pecan Sands (page 169)

Salami Crisps (page 218)

Mom's Perfect Tomato Sandwiches (page 107)

You can make a cocktail party as fancy or as casual as you like. I give some details for how to make it a little swanky if the occasion calls for it, but a couple dozen ham biscuits and a few bottles of Champagne, and as far as I'm concerned you've got yourself a cocktail party suitable for church clothes or flip-flops. The rest is purely optional.

And options can be fun. When I have the time and I want to host a party that goes a little beyond the everyday, I have a few guidelines I follow to help me make sure everyone feels at home and has a good time.

I try to set the tone right from the start so that when guests walk in, they immediately feel at home but also feel as if there's something a little special in the air. I have a signature drink ready and waiting to greet them, I have the lighting down low to give the setting an intimate vibe, and I make sure I'm serving as a good role model by having fun myself. To accomplish this last part, I try to plan and do as much ahead of time as I can. I've included my typical planning to-do list below that you can use and adapt as you see fit.

Another key to happy hostessing for me is not taking on every single detail myself. I am perfectly fine not being Superwoman. Figure out what you're comfortable delegating or purchasing and what you want to concentrate on doing yourself. That way you avoid spreading yourself too thin. A happy hostess makes for happy guests, but a frazzled hostess makes guests uncomfortable and awkward. So do everyone a favor and do as much as you can before the party begins and be willing to delegate some of the duties so you can work the party rather than have it working you.

MY COCKTAIL PARTY TO-DO LIST

• Plan and prepare the food. Choose only pick-up food that doesn't require utensils so that neither you nor your guests have to worry about plates and forks. It's awkward to eat standing up from even a small plate, so keep the food bite-size with only a cocktail napkin necessary. When serving biscuits with meat inside, be sure to chop the meat into tiny pieces so there's no big piece of meat that could be difficult to chew through or that could fall out and onto your party dress. Not elegant.

• Pick a signature drink. This is a small detail that goes a long way in setting the mood and tone for a party. My—or should I say John's—recipe for the Morey Margarita (page 238) is one John came up with all on his own as a signature drink for the surprise fortieth birthday party he threw for me. He created the drink for the party, gave the recipe to the bar service, and arranged for a bartender to stand in the driveway with one on a silver tray, waiting for me when I arrived. My friends told me John could not contain himself waiting for me to get there—they described him as a "lovesick puppy."

• A signature drink doesn't have to make a splash as dramatic as a bartender with a silver tray in the driveway, and it doesn't have to be an original recipe you come up with all on your own (although

I do have to say I was pretty smitten by John's execution), but you can apply the same idea to any party. As the guests arrive, have a special concoction already assembled and ready for them to pick up and try. It doesn't take a whole lot of extra time or preparation and yet it makes your guests feel special, it provides a conversation piece to get the party started, and in general it sends the signal that the night calls for something a little outside the same old same old. The night of my party was certainly out of the ordinary and caught me by complete surprise—and when I want to relive it, I ask John to whip me up a Morey Margarita (page 238), or as I now like to call it, a Lovesick Puppy.

• Make a music playlist that fits the party. Give this one some thought. Will this be a sedate party honoring someone, or could this potentially break into a dance party? Pick music that reflects the mood you want the party to radiate.

• Consider hiring some helpers. I like my cocktail parties to have good energy, with people moving about from room to room rather than everyone camped out in a dining room where all the food is on one table and the lights are on full blast. I often hire a few of the girls' babysitters to pass the food around on trays rather than having static groupings of food that tend to encourage clumping of people.

• Consider hiring a bartender. Again, this could be a college student working for pocket money, or you could hire a bartending service. I usually set up a self-serve bar, but sometimes a large or special party calls for extra hands.

• Rent glassware. Renting glasses from a party rental company is surprisingly inexpensive. The glasses come in a rack that you can pick up yourself. Then you can stow the rack out the back door or in your laundry room during the party, and as glasses are used, you simply return them to the rack. Take the full rack back to the rental company without even having to clean the glasses! One of my favorite shortcuts.

• Order desserts. For me, I find that making small, elegant desserts appropriate for a cocktail party is too time consuming. I'd rather focus on my other food. So I often order desserts ahead of time. I usually group the sweets in a static place where people can pick them up. I like to order petits fours or scrumptious mini chocolate cakes by Chocolate Cake Charleston. I really don't think I could make anything better myself. If you'd like to offer a larger selection of sweets, consider adding Pecan Sands (page 169) or store-bought or homemade brownies or fudge cut in bite-size cubes. Or make pecan tassies in mini muffin tins with piecrust dough (see page 147) and Drunk and Toasty Myers Pecan Pie filling (see page 152). I usually put out some fruit for people to eat with the sweets as well, because it's pretty.

• Put votive candles everywhere and turn the lights down low. I probably have close to 500 votive candles. A few days before the party I put them all over the house. Any ledge, any surface—votives. On the porch, on the bar, in the bathroom. It is such an inexpensive way to make a beautiful atmosphere. Set them out ahead of time and then put a long lighter close by so you're not searching for it minutes before the party. Then before the party starts, dim the overheard lights and let the candles do their magic.

- Make small flower arrangements. Similar to what I describe in the sit-down dinner preparations, I like to do very small arrangements in silver mint julep cups or mason jars, anything that is small and will reflect the light from the flickering votives.
- Turn down the temperature on the air conditioner . . . and then put a fire in the fireplace. A good couple of hours before the party begins, turn the temperature down, because the house will get warm as it fills with people. If it's at all possible, I have a fire going. It's the perfect touch of atmosphere that gives off the feeling of a warm, inviting home. This is one of those details that uses something you already have in your home, requires relatively little effort, and yet makes a big impression. You'll inspire your guests to rediscover their own fireplaces.
- Have lots of cocktail napkins on hand. At the bar, with the food, with the people passing food, with the desserts—cocktail napkins are multifunctional. I've mentioned that I collect linen cocktail napkins, but you can also buy new ones relatively inexpensively. If you entertain a good bit, you'll find you use them over and over again like the votive candles.
- Plan a catch-all area, such as a laundry room or pantry, that has a door where you can toss things or hide a mess and close it off from the rest of the party. Party guests inevitably gather in the kitchen, so you don't want your kitchen to be a disaster area.
- Have a good cab company in mind and the phone number on hand in case any of the guests has *too much* fun.

MY BAR CHECKLIST

When I'm setting up a self-serve bar, my goal is to anticipate every need so that during the party no one has to ask me where's the corkscrew, do I have any tonic, is there a spoon to stir with? Be generous with the amounts of everything and have everything out in clear view—you want to seem bountiful and hospitable and, again, you do not want to have to be running around and cutting more limes to replenish the supply or getting more beer out of the garage beer fridge when you'd rather be enjoying spending time with your guests. Most everything at the bar is stuff you can use after the party—it's not going to go bad. So err on the side of too much rather than too little when it comes to the drink ingredients, garnishes, and ice. There's nothing my husband loves more than a cooler after a party that still has beer in it. He keeps it on the porch and replenishes the ice as the post-party week goes on until we've finished all the beer. Ice-cold beer from a cooler is so much better than beer from a fridge, and it feels like a treat to have it that way at home during the week. Or we use a full cooler of beer left over from a Friday or Saturday night gathering as an excuse to have a "Sunday funday." Sunday afternoon oyster roast, anyone? So don't sweat the leftovers—enjoy them! Plan for three drinks per person when you're trying to figure how much alcohol you'll need.

A FEW DAYS BEFORE THE PARTY

• Find the best location for the bar. Choose a spot that's accessible but away from doorways and high-traffic areas so it doesn't impede the flow of the party. If there's a particular place where you'd like people to gather, that's where you want to put the bar.

• Set up a second small bar or beer cooler in the backyard, on the porch, or in the kitchen—wherever people are likely to gather that may be a little far from the main bar.

• Clean out pitchers for water and juice ahead of time so you're not doing this right before the party.

• Put a clean tablecloth on the bar if it's a card table or any other table you'd rather cover up.

• Put out a stack of cocktail napkins as well as a nice, crisp linen hand towel.

• Put out mixing spoons and the cocktail shaker.

• Put out a bottle opener for beer.

• Put out bottles of vodka, bourbon, Scotch, and gin.

• Put out bottles of tonic and soda.

• Put out glasses, lined up for easy access.

THE DAY OF THE PARTY

• Slice tons of lemons and limes and store in resealable plastic bags so that they are easy to replenish at the bar as needed.

• Prepare your signature drink and put in a pitcher.

• Set out lemons, limes, olives, and any garnishes related to your signature drink.

• Fill pitchers with water and freshly squeezed fruit juices.

• Put ice in a large crystal bowl, along with tongs. Have extra ice in a cooler close by or under the table.

• Have the beer on ice in the cooler.

• Open wine bottles so guests do not have to open them themselves. Put white wine and Champagne on ice in a bowl or other container. This is one way to use those galvanized tubs!

• Put out savory roasted pecans at the bar.

• Transition from project manager mode to party-goer mode. Make sure your demeanor reflects festivity and fellowship rather than "woman on a mission." Enjoy the fruits of your labor and the company of your friends. There's nothing wrong with the hostess having the most fun of anyone at the party. Or at least I should hope not!

Here's what's cookin'
Recipe from the kitchen of

Serves

Haystack

12 oz butter-scotch morsels
1-3 oz Chow Mein Noodles
Pecans or unsalted Nuts
about 1 cup

Melt morsels on top of st
Take off heat - add

Makes 6 to 8 servings

Coarse, kosher, or rock salt
6 dozen shucked oysters
¾ cup cooked, drained, and
    minced bacon

¾ cup minced green onions
    (about 6 onions, white and
    green parts)
1½ cups grated Gruyère cheese

Freshly ground black pepper

CAST-IRON ROASTED OYSTERS

You will need 36 oyster shell halves, preferably the rounded cup half.

1 Preheat the oven to 425°F. Pour a layer of salt into a cast-iron skillet. Nestle the oyster shells in the salt. You may have to do this in batches or use more than one skillet.

2 Divide the oysters among the shells, 2 oysters per shell. Top each with 1 teaspoon bacon, 1 teaspoon green onion, and 2 teaspoons cheese. Give each oyster a few grinds of black pepper.

3 Roast until the cheese melts and is bubbly and slightly browned, 8 to 10 minutes.

There's a funny story behind this delicious baked crab dish. And the story continues because I still get calls about this, almost five years later. My mother and I were scheduled to appear on the *Today* show for a segment about making homemade biscuits. Strictly for presentation, we needed an item that would be placed in the foreground on the set. At the last minute we decided on this crab dish because it freezes well and it's easy to transport. It was going to be the equivalent of a bowl of lemons or a basket of tomatoes and garlic sitting on the counter.

We go on air, and my mother happens to spoon a little of the crab onto a biscuit to hand to Hoda. Hoda puts it in her mouth and then looks over at Kathie Lee, wide-eyed like she's about to start moaning and groaning. "Kathie, wait until you taste this." And she is not talking about the biscuits—which were the whole point of us being

CALLIE'S
498 MEETING STREET CRAB

10 tablespoons (1¼ sticks) butter
¼ cup all-purpose flour
1 teaspoon dry mustard
½ teaspoon cayenne pepper
Kosher salt and freshly ground
    black pepper
2 cups whipping cream

3 shallots, minced
½ teaspoon Worcestershire sauce
¼ cup dry sherry or Marsala
    wine
1 pound lump crabmeat, picked
    over to be sure it's free of shell
    and cartilage

½ cup shredded cheddar cheese
½ cup chopped fresh chives
4 slices white bread
Serving suggestion: Crackers, hot
    biscuits

1 Preheat the oven to 375°F. Butter a 2-quart casserole dish with 1 tablespoon of the butter.
2 Melt 4 tablespoons of the butter in a saucepan. Whisk in the flour and cook until golden, 3 to 5 minutes. Whisk in the mustard, cayenne, ½ teaspoon salt, and ¼ teaspoon pepper.
3 In a separate small saucepan, warm the cream and then whisk it into the flour mixture.

4 In a small skillet, sauté the shallots in 1 tablespoon of the butter until soft, 4 to 6 minutes. Add to the sauce. Stir in the Worcestershire and sherry. Cook over low heat, stirring, until thick.
5 Fold in the crabmeat, cheddar cheese, and ¼ cup of the chives. Taste and adjust the salt and pepper. Pour into the casserole dish.

6 Pulse the bread in a food processor to make bread-crumbs. Melt the remaining 4 tablespoons butter. Mix in the crumbs. Sprinkle the crumbs and the remaining ¼ cup chives over the casserole. Bake about 30 minutes, until the top is golden brown and bubbling.
7 Serve with crackers or biscuits.

there. My poor mother is going on about the biscuits while Hoda and Kathie Lee are having an all-out fit over the crab: "Oh my gosh!" "These are unbelievable!" "Good night, Irene!" Their reaction to the crab dip was borderline obscene. We did receive a lot of responses about biscuits, but we got almost 500 calls and e-mails from all over the country wanting to know the crab recipe or wanting us to make the crab and send it to them.

And the callers were willing to make their case along the lines of "My grandson is having his bar mitzvah in a month, and we have to have that, we just have to have that."

So here it is: the recipe that about sent Hoda and Kathie Lee over the edge on live TV.

Makes 2½ cups, 6 to 8 appetizer portions or 4 side dish portions

BACON–GREEN ONION SAVORY CRISPS

Makes 24 pieces

2 tablespoons butter, melted, plus
 more for the baking sheet
12 slices bacon

6 green onions, coarsely
 chopped
⅔ cup crumbled feta cheese
¾ cup grated Parmesan cheese

4 (8 by 12-inch) sheets phyllo
 dough, thawed according to
 the package directions
Freshly ground black pepper

1 Preheat the oven to 375°F. Line a baking sheet with parchment paper and butter the parchment.
2 Cook the bacon until crispy. Remove the bacon to a paper bag to drain, leaving the drippins in the pan. When cool, crumble the bacon into a bowl.
3 Gently wilt the green onions in the bacon drippins. Drain on a paper bag, then add to the bacon. Mix in the feta and Parmesan to make the topping.

4 Lay a sheet of phyllo on the prepared baking sheet and brush with the melted butter. Sprinkle one-third of the topping on the sheet, all the way to the edges. Add a few grinds of pepper.
5 Top with another sheet of phyllo, brush with butter, sprinkle with half the remaining topping, and add pepper. Repeat once more with another phyllo sheet, butter, and the

remaining topping. Cover with the last sheet of phyllo and brush with butter.
6 Bake 12 to 15 minutes, until browned and crisp. Let cool for a minute.
7 Remove to a cutting board. Using a pizza cutter or serrated knife, cut into four 2-inch-wide strips. Then cut each strip into six 2-inch squares. Serve warm or at room temperature.

TUNA TARTARE

Makes 2½ cups, 4 appetizer portions or 40 (1-tablespoon) hors d'oeuvre portions

1 pound sashimi-grade tuna, well chilled
⅓ cup fresh lime juice
Grated zest of 1 lime
¼ to ½ teaspoon wasabi powder
1 to 2 teaspoons Asian chili paste

1½ tablespoons soy sauce
¼ cup vegetable oil
1 teaspoon toasted sesame oil
2 teaspoons unseasoned rice vinegar
2 tablespoons sesame seeds
1 avocado, pitted, peeled, and diced
4 green onions, chopped (white and green parts)

½ bunch cilantro, leaves only, chopped

SERVING SUGGESTIONS
Fried wonton skins
Rice crackers
Endive leaves
Cucumber rounds

1 Dice the tuna into small ¼-inch dice. Place in a chilled bowl, cover, and refrigerate.
2 Mix together the lime juice and zest, wasabi powder, chili paste, soy sauce, vegetable and sesame oils, and rice vinegar. Adjust the seasonings to your taste—you want a spicy mixture.

3 Toast the sesame seeds in a small dry skillet over medium heat for about 5 minutes, or until they smell fragrant and look golden in color. Set aside to cool.
4 Add the avocado, green onions, and cilantro to the tuna. Pour on the dressing and fold

gently to combine. Cover and refrigerate at least 1 hour to allow the flavors to marry.
5 Before serving, top with the sesame seeds. Serve with wonton skins, rice crackers, endive leaves, or cucumber rounds.

Makes 13 to 15 bruschetta pieces

SHRIMP
1 tablespoon olive oil
Grated zest of 1 lemon
Juice of ½ lemon
½ teaspoon kosher salt
¼ teaspoon freshly ground black
  pepper
⅛ teaspoon cayenne pepper
1 pound large shrimp (26 to 30
  count), peeled and deveined

5 or 6 skewers, soaked in water
  if wood or bamboo

DRESSING
6 tablespoons olive oil
3 tablespoons rice vinegar
1 tablespoon lemon juice, or
  more to taste
Grated zest of 1 lemon
3 green onions, minced (white
  and green parts)

1 clove garlic, minced
½ teaspoon dry mustard
Kosher salt

1 French baguette
Olive oil
2 cups arugula leaves, washed
  and dried
Kosher salt and freshly ground
  black pepper
Parmesan cheese wedge

SHRIMP BRUSCHETTA

This recipe requires a grill or stovetop grill pan.

1 Make the shrimp: Combine the olive oil, lemon zest and juice, salt, pepper, and cayenne in a resealable plastic bag. Add the shrimp and marinate 20 minutes.

2 Drain the shrimp and put 5 or 6 shrimp on each skewer. Refrigerate until you're ready to cook them.

3 Make the dressing: Combine all the ingredients in a jar. Cap tightly and shake to blend. Adjust to your taste for tartness with lemon juice and salt. Shake again well before using.

4 Heat a grill or grill pan. Cut the baguette into 13 to 15 (½-inch) slices and brush olive oil on both sides. Grill the bread until toasted. Arrange on a platter.

5 Toss the arugula in a bowl with 2 to 3 tablespoons of the dressing; do not soak the greens.

Taste and season with salt and pepper.

6 Grill the shrimp skewers 1 minute or less per side, just until pink and opaque. Remove the shrimp from the skewers.

7 Place a few arugula leaves on each bread slice and top with 2 shrimp. Use a vegetable peeler to shave a few thin strips of Parmesan on top.

SAVORY ROASTED PECANS

Nuts can be very expensive, but they last forever in the freezer, so I buy them less expensively in bulk during the harvest season and pull them out when I need them.

Makes about 2 cups

16 ounces pecan halves
6 tablespoons (¾ stick) butter, melted
½ teaspoon kosher salt

½ teaspoon freshly ground black pepper
½ teaspoon crushed red pepper flakes

½ teaspoon chili powder
¼ teaspoon sweet paprika
¼ teaspoon ground cumin

1 Preheat the oven to 350°F.
2 Coat the pecans in the butter. Combine the salt, pepper, red pepper, chili powder, paprika, and cumin in a heavy paper bag. Add the pecans and shake to coat well.
3 Spread the nuts on a baking sheet and roast in the oven for about 10 minutes, until lightly browned and fragrant.
4 Let cool and store in an airtight container.

Note: For a smoky flavor, add ½ teaspoon smoked paprika to the seasonings. You can also use the same process and substitute different spices to fit the theme of your party or the rest of your menu. For example, use grated lemon zest and thyme leaves instead of the spicy ingredients, or use coriander instead of cumin and substitute pistachios for the pecans.

Throw-Together Oyster Roast

MENU

Oysters (see The Basics, page 206)

Lemon Garlic Butter (page 208)

Cocktail Sauce (page 208)

Chimichurri Sauce (page 209)

Little League Chili (page 210)

Hot dogs

Frito Pie (page 210)

Pimento cheese sandwiches

Cast-Iron Pimento Cheese Dip (page 211)

Crab Crisps with Fresh Tomato Relish (page 212)

ADDITIONAL OR ALTERNATE RECIPES

Homemade French Onion Dip (page 77)

Pickled Shrimp (page 227)

Here's what my father—a lifelong Lowcountry boy—has to say about oyster roasts: All you need is oysters and friends. I take that guidance to heart, and nearly all of my oyster roasts are thrown together on pretty cool-weather days, a spontaneous "Sunday funday." I call Crosby's seafood, and if they've got fresh oysters, the party's on.

Traditionally, oyster roasts occur only within the months that have the letter *R* in them to reflect the oyster-harvesting season. But both ends of the season in the Lowcountry are a little iffy because of the heat, so instead of September through April, the months of October through March are really your best bet in the South. It goes without saying that an oyster roast is the ultimate in simple and casual entertaining—the shucking and eating are activity, meal, and conversation piece all in one. The party is all outdoors, so your house doesn't need to be spotless, and no decorations are necessary. Kids are welcome and can run around outside to their hearts' content. Since it's all self-serve food and drinks, you, the host, can really enjoy yourself at your own party. Still, there are a few details I like to add when I have the time, including snacks such as Boiled Peanuts (page 218) and Cast-Iron Pimento Cheese Dip (page 211) and food for those who don't eat oysters (and for those who like to eat oysters *and more*). I usually put out chili, hot dogs, and Frito Pie (page 210) with plenty of toppings or Slow Cooker Pulled Pork (see page 90) with buns, fresh pickles, coleslaw, and extra sauce. My dad would accuse me of being way too fancy with additions like these. Yes, Frito pie, too fancy!

THE BASICS: THE OYSTERS

- Large fire pit with raised sides or an improvised fire pit with cinder blocks around it
- In lieu of a fire, a jumbo-size steamer pot on an outdoor propane burner
- Large metal plate to go over the fire
- Heavy-duty work gloves for lifting the plate
- Burlap sacks the oysters come in—or loose burlap if they do not come in bags—to cover the oysters while they roast
- Water hose nearby for rinsing the oysters and soaking the burlap
- Cotton work gloves, rags, or old towels cut in strips for handling the heat and the sharp edges of the oysters
- Oyster knives for prying open the oysters, dipping the oysters into butter and sauces, and lifting them into your mouth
- Saltines brushed with butter and spices or herbs and then toasted. I serve these in a basket lined with burlap.
- Lemon Garlic Butter (page 208) and Cocktail Sauce (page 208) are essential, but you can also make other sauces as well, such as chimichurri (see page 209). I like to serve sauces in wide-mouth 4-ounce mason jars for easy dipping.
- Oyster table. This can be as simple as a piece of plywood over two sawhorses. Some people cut two large holes in the plywood and instead of

sawhorses, support the table with two 32-gallon trash cans or 55-gallon drums. Oyster shells can be tossed into the holes, where they land in the trash cans. You can even use a picnic table covered in newspaper. You can be as creative, fancy, or basic as you like with the table.

• Camping-style lanterns for lighting if it gets dark. I put these right on the oyster table.

Save Your Shells

Keep a few oyster shells, rinse them well, and put them in the dishwasher to get them really clean. Once they're dry, you can store them in gallon-size resealable plastic bags. Use them at another party to serve roasted oysters (see page 194), oysters Rockefeller, or oysters on the half shell with mignonette. For a pretty presentation, spread rock salt on a platter or tray. Lay the oyster shells on top of the rock salt and garnish the platter with fresh herbs or flowers.

ROASTING OYSTERS OVER A FIRE

Cinder block enclosure for the
   fire, or a large fire pit with
   sturdy raised sides
Large metal plate or narrow grate

Water hose
1 bushel of oysters per 4 to 6
   people

Burlap sacks from the oysters or a
   few yards of heavy burlap
Heavy work gloves
Optional: Shovel

1 Build the fire and let it get hot.
2 Put the plate on top of the fire, resting on the cinder blocks or sides of the fire pit. Let the plate get hot. To test readiness, spray the plate with the hose. If the water sizzles, it's ready for the oysters.

3 Wash the oysters well with the hose. Drain. Dump the oysters on the plate (this may need to be done in batches). Cover the oysters with burlap. Soak the burlap with water from the hose.
4 Let the oysters cook 15 minutes, or until the shells open.

Remove the burlap with gloved hands or a shovel.
5 Pick up the metal plate with gloved hands and then dump the oysters on the oyster table.

207

ROASTING OYSTERS
OVER A PROPANE BURNER

Jumbo-size steamer pot with steamer basket and lid
Heavy-duty propane burner and tank
1 bushel of oysters per 4 to 6 people
Water hose
Heavy work gloves

1 Pour 1 inch of water into the pot. Place over the burner and bring to a boil on high heat.
2 Wash the oysters well with the hose. Drain. Dump the oysters in the steamer basket. Place the basket in the pot and cover.
3 Steam the oysters for 5 minutes if you prefer wet and juicy oysters, and a few minutes more for drier. For drier oysters, the oysters are ready when the shells pop open just a little.
4 Turn off the burner. Wearing heavy gloves, uncover the pot and remove the basket. Dump the oysters on the oyster table.

LEMON GARLIC BUTTER

Makes about 2 cups

1 pound (4 sticks) butter
1 clove garlic, cut in half
Grated zest of 1 lemon
Kosher salt and freshly ground black pepper

Melt the butter in a small saucepan. Stir in the garlic and lemon zest. Season with salt and pepper. Simmer over low heat for 5 minutes. Fish out the garlic, if you wish, before serving the butter as a warm sauce.

COCKTAIL SAUCE

Makes about ¾ cup

½ cup ketchup
3 tablespoons prepared horseradish
2 teaspoons fresh lemon juice
½ teaspoon Worcestershire sauce
¼ teaspoon hot sauce
Optional: ¼ teaspoon sriracha (Asian chili sauce)

Mix all the ingredients and refrigerate.

CHIMICHURRI SAUCE

Makes about 3 cups

2 cups loosely packed chopped
    fresh cilantro
1 cup loosely packed chopped
    fresh flat-leaf parsley
5 cloves garlic, coarsely chopped

3 green onions, coarsely
    chopped (white and green
    parts)
½ jalapeño chile, seeded and
    coarsely chopped

Juice of ½ lime
½ cup red wine vinegar
1 cup olive oil
Kosher salt and freshly ground
    black pepper

Place the cilantro, parsley, garlic, green onions, and jalapeño in a food processor and pulse a few times. Add the lime juice and vinegar and pulse to combine. With the machine running, slowly add the olive oil and process until sauce-like. Season to taste with salt and pepper.

THE EXTRAS

• Chili, hot dogs, and Frito Pie (page 210). I put out hot dogs, buns, ketchup and mustard, sour cream, shredded cheese, chopped onions, sliced jalapeño chiles, and individual bags of Fritos.

• Slow Cooker Pulled Pork with Vinegar-Based BBQ Sauce (page 90). If you have access to an electrical outlet outside or have an extension cord, you can keep the BBQ warm in the slow cooker and people can serve themselves as they feel like it. Make sure you have buns, Grandmama's Fresh Pickles (page 111), Childhood Southern Cole Slaw (page 132), and plenty of extra BBQ sauce alongside.

• Boiled Peanuts (page 218). I use two galvanized buckets or small tubs to serve—one to hold the peanuts and one for the discarded shells.

• Pimento cheese sandwiches. You can make these ahead of time and put them out on the table with the chili and dogs.

• Cast-Iron Pimento Cheese Dip (page 211). Carry the skillet outside and serve right from it with a burlap-lined basket of tortilla chips alongside for dipping. You can even reheat this by putting the skillet on the metal oyster plate over the fire.

• Crab Crisps with Fresh Tomato Relish (page 212), because you can never have enough seafood! If you make homemade tortillas for the crisps, you can make more than needed and use them for the pimento cheese dip.

• Self-serve s'mores. After the fire is finished with its oyster-roasting duties, or if there is another fire pit or outdoor fireplace available, put out wooden skewers and baskets of marshmallows, chocolate bars, and graham crackers and let your guests make s'mores or roast marshmallows at their leisure.

LITTLE LEAGUE CHILI

Makes 12 (½-cup) servings

1 tablespoon vegetable oil
1½ pounds ground beef
1 pound ground pork
2 tablespoons chili powder
2 tablespoons Worcestershire sauce
1 tablespoon hot sauce
2 teaspoons minced garlic

1 teaspoon dry mustard
1 teaspoon garlic powder
1 teaspoon onion powder
1½ cups ketchup
¾ cup yellow mustard
3 tablespoons water

Heat the oil on medium heat in a deep cast-iron skillet or large saucepan. Brown the meat, using the back of a spoon to break it into little pieces. Add the remaining ingredients and stir well. Reduce the heat to low and simmer 30 minutes, or until thickened. Add a little more water for less thickness and to make it more sauce-like. Serve on hot dogs, in Frito Pie (recipe follows), or on its own with toppings.

FRITO PIE

Makes 1 serving

1 single-serve bag Fritos Original Corn Chips
½ cup warm chili (such as Little League Chili, above)
½ cup shredded cheddar cheese
2 tablespoons chopped onion
1 tablespoon chopped jalapeño chile, or more to taste

OPTIONAL TOPPINGS
Diced tomatoes, plain or with green chiles (if canned), sour cream, diced avocado, sliced green onion, shredded lettuce, chopped pitted olives, sliced radishes, sliced fresh jalapeño chiles

Split open a Fritos bag down the side of the package. Spoon on the chili, cheese, onion, pepper, and toppings of your choice and dig in.

Variation: Instead of using individual bags of Fritos, empty a large bag into a serving bowl and put out bowls (or waxed paper bags) so people can make Frito pies with their choice of toppings.

CAST-IRON PIMENTO CHEESE DIP

Makes 14 to 16 servings

8 to 12 ounces fresh chorizo
sausage, casing removed
1 (16-ounce) container pimento
cheese (your favorite, preferably spicy)

2 cups Southern Staple Salsa
(page 87) or 1 (16-ounce)
container good-quality pico de
gallo or salsa
Serving suggestion: Corn tortilla
chips

Garnish (optional): Fresh cilantro leaves, chopped red bell
pepper.

1 Crumble the chorizo into a
cast-iron skillet. Using a fork
to break up the sausage, cook
6 to 8 minutes, until browned.
If it seems very greasy, spoon
off the fat. Stir in the pimento
cheese and salsa and cook

over low heat until the cheese
is melted and combined well
and the dip is heated through.
Serve hot from the skillet with
tortilla chips. Garnish with
cilantro or red pepper, if you
wish.

2 If you need to reheat, put back
to remelt on a warm burner,
outdoor grill, or metal oyster
plate over the fire while the
oysters are cooking.

CRAB CRISPS WITH FRESH TOMATO RELISH

Makes 4 dozen crisps and 1½ cups tomato relish

FRESH TOMATO RELISH
1 pound tomatoes
½ cup chopped white onion
1 cup loosely packed chopped fresh cilantro
3 tablespoons fresh lime juice
1 teaspoon olive oil

Kosher salt and freshly ground black pepper
2 dashes hot sauce, or more to taste

CRAB CRISPS
1 or 2 avocados

Juice of ½ lime
Kosher salt
½ pound fresh lump crabmeat, picked over to be sure it's free of shell and cartilage
Tortilla chips (see Note)

1 Make the fresh tomato relish: Peel (see page 157) and chop the tomatoes. Add the onion, cilantro, lime juice, olive oil, ¾ teaspoon salt, and pepper to taste. Refrigerate for 1 hour. (This makes more than you will need. Use the extra as a relish on sandwiches or salads, as a dip served with chips or veggies, or stuffed in half of an avocado.) Taste and adjust the salt. Add the hot sauce.

2 Make the crab crisps: Pit, peel, and slice the avocado. Sprinkle with lime juice and kosher salt. Gently break up the crabmeat in a separate bowl. To assemble, put 1 teaspoon tomato relish on a chip. Top with 1 teaspoon crabmeat and a slice of avocado.

Note: Be sure the tortilla chips you buy can hold the topping, or make your own—see page 95 for home-made tortilla strips, but cut the tortillas into triangles instead of strips.

THE DRINKS

• I set up a Bloody Mary bar outside or on the porch with a pitcher of premixed Beer Bloodies (page 234) and olives, celery sticks, lemon and lime wedges, and small wooden skewers with small boiled shrimp and cherry tomatoes. You can put out glasses or mason jars and everyone can serve themselves.

• I use a galvanized tub of ice with beer, Champagne, and white wine. We have a wall-mounted bottle opener on our back porch; that may be a home improvement project worth doing! No matter what, make sure you have a bottle opener near the tub of beer and open up the bottles of wine ahead of time.

• I always place a recycling bin nearby for empty beer and wine bottles.

Game Day

MENU

Lemon-Thyme Chicken Wings (page 216)

Boiled Peanuts (page 218)

Salami Crisps (page 218)

Asparagus Bacon Roll-Ups (page 221)

Fiery Cheese Wafers (page 221)

Homemade French Onion Dip (page 77)

DILLicious Cucumber Sandwiches (page 108)

ADDITIONAL OR ALTERNATE RECIPES

Cast-Iron Pimento Cheese Dip (page 211)

Assorted biscuits (pages 17, 20, and 22)

Fiery Pimento Cheese–Laced "Naughty" Eggs (page 114)

Pimento cheese sandwiches or serve with crackers

Whether we're tailgating at a Carolina Gamecocks football game or watching the whole day's slate of college football at home on TV from noon until the West Coast teams finish up, every Saturday in the fall is Game Day. This is another one of those fun opportunities to socialize while doing an activity. Some people may not consider watching football an "activity" per se, but for most of us in the South, the spectating, tailgating, and cheering is a rigorous sport in itself, accompanied—of course—by delicious food and drink that make us root with that much more gusto.

When we tailgate at a Carolina game, perhaps it's a testament to how seriously we take our football that we all dress up as if we're going to church. Dresses, nice shoes—and the jewels come out, too. One time, my friend Krysten's California husband and I were talking about their plans to join us for a game. I said, "And don't forget, we dress up." I didn't want him to feel uncomfortable if he showed up in shorts and a t-shirt. "Dress up as what?" he asked. He thought I meant costumes,

like a gamecock costume! When we make the trip to the "cocktail party in the concrete jungle," we don't scrimp on our makeup or hair, or on the food and drinks.

All of these recipes work well for hosting a Game Day get-together at your house. While some travel better than others, if you're thinking about packing them up for a real tailgate, I would save the Asparagus Bacon Roll-Ups (page 221) for an at-home party. But a great idea for an easy-to-tote treat is to make mini macaroni bites. Make Caroline's Macaroni Pie (page 70). Chill it in the fridge, then use a biscuit cutter to cut the casserole into individual round pieces of macaroni-and-cheese goodness. Serve with toothpicks for picking up the macaroni bites.

As far as decorating, I don't decorate for tailgating. Between the Carolina garnet and black we're all wearing and the abundance of food, drinks, and coolers erupting from the backs of the cars into the parking lot, no further embellishment is needed. In fact, it might just result in sensory overload.

LEMON-THYME CHICKEN WINGS

Double, triple, or quadruple this recipe to keep the rabid fans fed!

Makes 12 wings

Grated zest and juice of 2 lemons (about ½ cup juice)
2 tablespoons olive oil
4 large cloves garlic, minced

¼ white onion, minced
1½ teaspoons minced fresh thyme
1½ teaspoons kosher salt

½ teaspoon cayenne pepper
12 chicken wings, split
Garnish (optional): Chopped green onions

1 Combine the lemon zest and juice, olive oil, garlic, onion, thyme, salt, and cayenne in a resealable plastic bag. Add the wings. Refrigerate overnight, and whenever you open the fridge, turn the bag to coat the wings.

2 When you're ready to cook, preheat the oven to 350°F.
3 Put the wings in a single layer in a baking pan or skillet and pour the marinade over them. Bake 30 minutes.

4 Turn the oven to broil. Broil the wings 3 minutes on one side; turn and broil 5 minutes on the other side, or until brown and crispy. Garnish with chopped green onions, if you wish.

BOILED PEANUTS

These can be frozen; reheat in the microwave.

Makes 9½ cups

5 quarts cold water
½ cup kosher salt
2 pounds green peanuts,
  washed, shells on

1 Combine the water and salt in a large stockpot and bring to a boil. Add the peanuts. Cover and keep at a slow boil for 1 hour.
2 After the hour, take a few peanuts out to taste for doneness. A boiled peanut will have the texture of a soft bean—not the shell, that is, but the nut inside.
3 Reduce the heat to a simmer and check every 30 minutes for softness until they reach your preferred texture. This might take up to 1½ hours or longer. Drain well.
4 Enjoy while warm, at room temperature, or cold if you prefer.
5 Pack in resealable plastic bags to store in the fridge or freeze.

SALAMI CRISPS

I ask the person at the deli counter to slice the salami paper thin.

Makes 80 pieces

1 (16-ounce) container sour cream
1 cup minced fresh basil, plus 20 fresh basil leaves cut in chiffonade (may want to use a mini food processor to mince this amount of basil)

2 to 3 teaspoons minced garlic
½ teaspoon kosher salt
½ to 1 teaspoon crushed red pepper flakes
½ pound salami, sliced to yield 80 slices

80 pieces shaved Parmesan cheese

1 Mix the sour cream, minced basil, garlic, salt, and red pepper to taste. Refrigerate for at least 1 hour or overnight to allow the flavors to marry.
2 Preheat the oven to 300°F.
3 Cut the salami into paper-thin rounds if you did not have the deli do it for you. Spread in a single layer on an ungreased baking sheet and crisp in the oven. Look for the edges to begin to darken and crisp up, 15 to 25 minutes. Remove and drain on a paper bag.
4 Adjust the seasonings in the sour cream to your taste; the salami crisps are salty.
5 To assemble: Place the salami crisps on a platter, top each with a dollop of seasoned sour cream and a small piece of Parmesan, and sprinkle the platter with the chiffonade of basil.

Variation: For an alternate presentation, make the sour cream dip (adding the basil chiffonade), bake the crisps, and serve the salami as chips to dip into the sour cream.

Chiffonade

Chiffonade is an easy and pretty method of cutting leafy herbs and greens. Stack a few leaves, one on top of another. Roll up along a long edge, cigar-style, then use a very sharp knife to make thin cross-cuts through the stack. Gently separate into ribbons.

ASPARAGUS BACON ROLL-UPS

Makes 16 pieces (recipe can easily be doubled or tripled)

1 (8-ounce) block cream cheese, at room temperature
½ cup grated Parmesan cheese
3 teaspoons finely minced garlic
1½ tablespoons fresh lemon juice
¼ teaspoon kosher salt
⅛ teaspoon freshly ground black pepper
32 spears asparagus, trimmed
16 slices bacon
16 slices white bread
4 tablespoons (½ stick) butter, melted

1 Beat together the cream cheese, Parmesan, garlic, lemon juice, salt, and pepper. (This can be made a day in advance and refrigerated.)
2 Preheat the oven to 400°F.
3 Bring a large pot of salted water to a boil. Blanch the asparagus in the boiling water for 1 minute. Drain and place in a bowl of ice water until cold. Drain the asparagus well and dry each spear.

4 Partially cook the bacon, keeping it limber, as you will wrap the bread with it. Remove to a paper bag to drain.
5 Use a serrated knife to remove the crusts from the bread. (Save them to make breadcrumbs, if you like.) Flatten each bread slice with a rolling pin. Spread each slice of bread with the cream cheese mixture. Place 2 asparagus spears in the center of the bread, from one corner to another. Pick up a free corner and roll. Wrap each roll-up with a piece of bacon and secure with a toothpick.
6 Place the roll-ups on a baking sheet. Use a pastry brush to brush the bread with the melted butter. Bake until golden brown, 12 to 15 minutes. Serve warm.

FIERY CHEESE WAFERS

Makes 4 dozen wafers

2 cups shredded sharp cheddar cheese
½ pound (2 sticks) butter, at room temperature
2 cups sifted all-purpose flour
½ teaspoon kosher salt
½ teaspoon cayenne pepper, or more to taste

1 Pulse the cheese in a food processor for 10 to 12 seconds. Add the butter and pulse to combine.
2 Sift the flour and whisk in the salt and cayenne. Mix the flour and cheese mixture together by hand until well combined.
3 Place 2 pieces of plastic wrap (each at least 16 inches long) on the work surface. Divide the dough in 2 pieces and place each on a piece of plastic wrap. Shape each into a log 12 inches long and 1 inch in diameter by rolling it back and forth on the counter. (If the dough is too soft, chill in the fridge.) Twist the ends of the plastic wrap to secure. Once shaped, chill the logs for 30 to 45 minutes, until quite firm.
4 Preheat the oven 350°F.
5 Slice each log into 24 slices, each ½ inch thick. Place on an ungreased baking sheet, ½ inch apart. Bake until golden, 12 to 15 minutes.
6 Let cool on a cooling rack. Pack the wafers in tins to keep them crisp.

Note: The logs can be frozen. When ready to use, remove them from freezer and set out. When soft enough, slice and prepare logs as directed above.

Variation: Use 1½ cups crumbled Gorgonzola cheese in place of the cheddar and add ½ cup chopped toasted pecans.

Southern Picnic

MENU

Pork Ribs with Brown Sugar–Bourbon BBQ Sauce (page 224)

South Fork Slaw (page 227)

Pickled Shrimp (page 227)

Reunion Fried Chicken (page 62)

Q's Potato Salad (page 133)

Peach Upside Down Cake (page 228)

ADDITIONAL OR ALTERNATE RECIPES

Mom's Perfect Tomato Sandwiches (page 107)

Egg salad sandwiches (see page 118)

Fiery Pimento Cheese–Laced "Naughty" Eggs (page 114)

Boiled Peanuts (page 218)

Frozen Fruit Kebobs (page 136)

You don't have to be in the South to create and experience the quintessential Southern picnic. In fact, my most memorable Southern picnic was actually one I put together for a float down the Teton River, winding through the picturesque Grand Teton Mountains. There were four adults and six children, so we floated down on a boat with a large raft tied behind so the children could have their "own" boat. We floated, fished, and stopped to swim as we felt like it. The children scrutinized every small island in the river in search of the perfect spot for us to get out and picnic. And when they "discovered" it, they named it appropriately for our menu: Rib Island. After we ate, we all jumped in the river to clean off all the drippy BBQ sauce. So I guess you could say this picnic is napkin-optional!

Another great menu for a picnic is Reunion Fried Chicken (page 62), Q's Potato Salad (page 133), and watermelon wedges. Enjoy the fried chicken at room/outdoor temperature or keep warm in a paper bag or in a cooler with other warm stuff. Tastes amazing hot or cold! And the Pickled Shrimp (page 227) stored in a mason jar makes a perfect take-along that can be nibbled along the way or with the meal.

SOUTHERN PICNIC TIPS

- Pick your menu with regard to space. This menu works well because the items pack well and each makes just the right amount of food—very filling but not requiring a lot of space to pack.
- Pick a menu with a minimum of paper products/ utensils needed. Dishes shouldn't take more than a paper plate to hold.
- Wrap sandwiches in parchment paper to keep them fresh but not soggy. Then put the wrapped sandwiches in a larger Tupperware container.
- Mix kosher salt and freshly ground black pepper together before the picnic and carry in one small container.
- Take a trash bag with you to stow all the trash.
- Mix up a batch of the Morey Margarita (page 238), Lime Berry Cooler (page 238), or Sweet Tea with Mint (page 242) and tote in a gallon milk container or other pouring container.

PORK RIBS WITH BROWN SUGAR–BOURBON BBQ SAUCE

Once the ribs come out of the oven, they are completely cooked and ready to eat. I add the grilling step to give the ribs a nice charred finish, but that's optional.

Makes 10 to 12 servings

3 racks pork ribs (about 36 ribs)
Kosher salt and freshly ground
   black pepper

1½ cups minced white onions
3 tablespoons minced garlic
Juice of 3 oranges

Juice of 3 limes
Brown Sugar–Bourbon BBQ
   Sauce (page 225)

1 Remove or have your butcher remove the rib membrane. That silvery fibrous piece needs to be removed so the marinade can flavor the meat; removing it also makes the meat easier to chew. Use a spoon or butter knife to lift the membrane from the edge of the rack. Once you loosen it, use a paper towel to grab on to it and pull it away. Do this to each of the racks.

2 Rub both sides of the racks with salt and pepper. Place the racks in a large roasting pan, overlapping as necessary. Combine the onions and garlic with the orange and lime juices and pour over the racks. Cover the pan with foil or plastic wrap and refrigerate overnight. If you do not have room in your refrigerator for a large pan, place the ribs and citrus marinade in one or more extra-large resealable plastic bags.

3 Preheat the oven to 225°F.

4 Let the meat come back to room temperature. Rub each rack with ½ cup of the BBQ sauce. Re-cover the pan with foil. Bake 2 hours 30 minutes to 3 hours.

5 Begin checking for doneness at the 2-hour point. To check if the ribs are done, grab a bone and see if it twists or moves when you pull on it. The bones should be visible and the ribs flexible.

6 If you choose to grill the ribs, prepare the grill while the ribs are in the oven, making sure the grates are clean and oiled. Lightly brush the racks with the BBQ sauce. Place on the grill and cook to crisp, about 3 minutes per side.

7 Use your kitchen shears to cut the racks into individual ribs. Serve with the sauce on the side.

8 To pack for a picnic, place each serving (about 3 ribs) on a large piece of heavy-duty foil and brush the top with a good bit of sauce. Wrap tightly. If you want to keep them warm, stow them in their own cooler—without any cold foods in the cooler, of course!

BROWN SUGAR–BOURBON BBQ SAUCE

This is a chunky sauce—I like it that way. But if you prefer a smoother sauce, you can let it cool and puree it in a blender.

Makes about 3 cups

2 tablespoons vegetable oil
2 cups minced yellow onions
3 tablespoons minced garlic
½ cup packed dark brown sugar
2 cups ketchup
⅓ cup bourbon
⅓ cup cider vinegar

¼ cup Dijon mustard
1 tablespoon Worcestershire
   sauce
2 teaspoons dry mustard
2 teaspoons sriracha (Asian chili
   sauce), Tabasco sauce, Texas
   Pete, or your favorite hot sauce

1 teaspoon chili powder
½ teaspoon ground cumin
Kosher salt and freshly ground
   black pepper

1 Heat the oil in a saucepan on medium heat. Add the onions and cook about 10 minutes, stirring occasionally, until golden brown.

2 Add the garlic and cook until the garlic is fragrant. Add the sugar and cook, stirring, until it melts, 6 to 8 minutes.

3 Stir in the remaining ingredients and simmer 20 to 30 minutes. Taste and adjust the salt and pepper.

225

SOUTH FORK SLAW

You can substitute 2 (16-ounce) containers store-bought refrigerated salsa or 4 cups Southern Staple Salsa (page 87) for the chopped tomato, onion, and cilantro.

You'll need 3½ to 4½ pounds whole cabbage, as 1 pound cabbage yields 3½ to 4½ cups shredded.

Makes 10 to 12 servings

12 to 15 cups shredded cabbage
⅓ cup white vinegar
½ teaspoon celery seeds
Ice water
5 tomatoes (about 1½ pounds), peeled (see page 157) and chopped

1 large red onion, diced
2 cups loosely packed fresh cilantro leaves
¾ cup mayonnaise
¼ cup olive oil
Juice of 1 lime
2 teaspoons kosher salt

2 or 3 jalapeño chiles, diced (remove the seeds if you prefer it less spicy)
3 avocados

1 Place the cabbage in a large bowl. Combine the vinegar and celery seeds and pour over the cabbage. Cover the cabbage with ice water. Refrigerate at least 2 hours or overnight.
2 Drain the cabbage well. Return it to the bowl and mix in the tomatoes, onion, and cilantro. Combine the mayonnaise, olive oil, lime juice, 2 teaspoons salt, and the jalapeños. Pour over the cabbage mixture and toss well to combine. Taste and adjust the salt. Refrigerate at least 1 hour to allow the flavors to marry.
3 Just before serving, peel, pit, and dice the avocados. Add to the slaw and mix through gently.

PICKLED SHRIMP

Makes 1 quart

8⅓ cups water
Kosher salt
2 pounds shrimp, peeled, tails left on, deveined
3 white onions, cut in half lengthwise and thinly sliced

1½ cups good-quality olive oil
2 cups cider vinegar
8 bay leaves
3 teaspoons crushed red pepper flakes
4 cloves garlic, cut in half

1½ lemons, thinly sliced, seeds removed
⅓ cup capers in brine, drained and rinsed
1½ teaspoons celery seeds

1 Bring 8 cups of the water and 6 tablespoons salt to a boil in a large saucepan. Add the shrimp and cook 2 minutes, just until the shrimp turn pink. Drain the shrimp and let cool.
2 Combine the remaining ⅓ cup water with all the remaining ingredients in a large bowl. Stir and add 1½ teaspoons salt. Stir, taste, and add more salt if necessary. Add the cooled shrimp, stir, cover, and refrigerate overnight.
3 To tote to a picnic, put in a mason jar for traveling and stow in a cooler. Serve with toothpicks or pick out the shrimp with your fingers—yum!

PEACH UPSIDE DOWN CAKE

This cake is inspired by Mama's pineapple upside down cake. It keeps well and can even be served in the morning as a coffee cake. It's just as good served at room temperature—perfect for packing and picnicking!

Makes 1 (9-inch) round cake

12 tablespoons (1½ sticks) butter, at room temperature
¾ cup packed light brown sugar
4 peaches (if you care to peel your peaches, see page 157 for an easy method)

1½ cups all-purpose flour
½ teaspoon ground cinnamon
2 teaspoons baking powder
¼ teaspoon kosher salt
1 cup white sugar
½ cup whole milk

2 large eggs
1 tablespoon maple syrup
1 teaspoon pure vanilla extract

1 Preheat the oven to 350°F.
2 Melt 4 tablespoons of the butter in a 9-inch cast-iron skillet. Remove from the heat and stir in the brown sugar.
3 Slice the peaches ½ inch thick. Making a circular pattern, place the slices flat side down to cover the bottom of the skillet.
4 Whisk together the flour, cinnamon, baking powder, and salt in a large bowl. In another bowl, beat the remaining 8 tablespoons butter and the white sugar with a handheld mixer until pale lemon colored. In a third bowl, combine the milk, eggs, maple syrup, and vanilla. Add the butter mixture to the flour mixture and mix on low speed. Stir in the milk mixture until a smooth batter forms. Pour the batter over the peaches and level with a spatula.
5 Bake 45 to 55 minutes, until a tester inserted in the center of the cake comes out clean and the top is golden brown and does not jiggle.
6 While hot, flip the cake onto a plate for presentation.

Playdate

MENU

ADDITIONAL OR ALTERNATE RECIPES

Even a playdate calls for good, fresh food. In fact, the more food, the better! Usually the playdate begins following morning preschool, so I make lunch ahead of time and have it ready when I pick the kids up and bring them to the house. No matter how many activities I plan for the girls and their guests, they seem to fly through them at an alarming pace. Painting on the porch with water colors or playing with homemade playdough are a couple of their favorite activities. I try to plan extra activities punctuated by lots of breaks for healthy snacks, and I also try to make snack time into an activity as well. The children can pick from toppings such as mini marshmallows, chocolate chips, and dried fruit for the granola and mix them into their own bowls. They can help listen out for the popcorn starting to pop and then starting to slow, and shake on their own seasonings. We can even make the playdough and they can add the ingredients and their favorite shade of food coloring.

For spend-the-night guests, Aunt Martha's Biscuit Doughnuts (page 44) make for a festive and entertaining breakfast, as does John's Puffy Pancake (page 164). You might wonder about the tuna casserole, but, let me tell you, I'm worn out by the end of a playdate. And I always have a tuna casserole in the freezer I can thaw for just those times when a playdate goes on a little too long and instead of concentrating on supper I'd rather be concentrating on an adult beverage.

MOREY GIRLS GRANOLA

Makes 8 to 10 cups

4 cups old-fashioned rolled oats (not quick-cooking)
1 cup sliced almonds
½ cup pecan halves
½ cup sunflower seeds
½ cup shredded sweetened coconut

½ cup maple syrup
¼ cup molasses
2 tablespoons raw sugar
1 teaspoon ground cinnamon
1 teaspoon kosher salt
1 teaspoon pure vanilla extract

1 cup dried fruit of your choice (Morey girls' favorites are raisins and dried cranberries)
½ cup mini chocolate chips
½ cup mini marshmallows

1 Preheat the oven to 350°F.
2 Combine the oats, almonds, pecans, sunflower seeds, coconut, maple syrup, molasses, sugar, cinnamon, salt, and vanilla in a large bowl. Mix well. Spread on a baking sheet. Bake 20 to 30 minutes, tossing the mixture every 10 minutes, until golden brown.

3 Remove from the oven and let cool to room temperature.
4 Stir in the dried fruit, chocolate chips, and marshmallows. Store in an airtight container.

POPCORN FOR PLAYDATES

Makes 30 (½-cup) servings

3 tablespoons olive oil
6-quart pan with a lid
¾ cup popcorn kernels

2 teaspoons kosher salt
2 to 4 tablespoons colored sprinkles

Heat the oil in a 6-quart (or larger) saucepan on high heat. Add the kernels and 1 teaspoon of the salt. Cover with the lid. When the kernels begin to pop (after about 2 minutes), shake the pan to distribute the kernels in an even layer. Cook, shaking the pan every now and then, until the rate of kernels popping slows down (about 5 minutes). Turn down the heat to medium and continue shaking the pan until the popping stops. Remove from the heat to avoid burning. Pour the popcorn into a large bowl and sprinkle with the remaining 1 teaspoon salt and the sprinkles.

HOMEMADE PLAYDOUGH

The cinnamon is just to make this smell good. I wouldn't recommend eating it, even though it won't hurt you!

Makes about 3 cups

2 cups all-purpose flour
½ cup kosher salt
2 cups water
2 tablespoons vegetable oil

¼ cup cream of tartar
1 teaspoon ground cinnamon
Food coloring

Mix all the ingredients in a saucepan, adding food coloring to the preferred shade of color. Stir over low to medium heat until the dough is no longer sticky. Let cool. Store in an airtight container or resealable plastic bag.

You can top this casserole with leftover biscuits for a yummy buttery crust or you can top with breadcrumbs. My husband grew up with crushed potato chip topping, so when we don't have any leftover biscuits, I usually top half with crushed potato chips for him and half with breadcrumbs for me.

Four ounces of dried pasta will cook up to about 2 cups, so you'll need about 5 ounces for this. When you cook the spaghetti, boil it about 2 minutes less than the suggested time; it will cook more when you bake it.

Makes 8 servings

TUNA CASSEROLE

3 tablespoons butter
4 (5-ounce) cans water-packed
    albacore tuna, drained
1 cup diced white onion
1 cup chopped celery
1 cup mayonnaise

Kosher salt and freshly ground
    black pepper
2½ cups cooked, drained
    spaghetti
1 tablespoon all-purpose flour
1 cup milk, warmed

2½ cups shredded Swiss cheese
About 6 leftover biscuits, split,
    or ½ cup dry breadcrumbs or
    crushed potato chips

1 Preheat the oven to 375°F. Butter a 2-quart casserole dish with 1 tablespoon of the butter.
2 Combine the tuna, onion, celery, and mayonnaise. Season with salt and pepper. Add the spaghetti and mix well.
3 Melt the remaining 2 tablespoons butter in a large saucepan on low heat. Whisk in the flour and cook 5 minutes, until the starchy taste is gone. Do not allow the flour to brown.
4 Add the tuna-spaghetti mixture, followed by the milk, 2 cups of the cheese, ½ teaspoon salt, and ¼ teaspoon pepper. Mix well. Pour into the casserole.
5 Sprinkle the remaining ½ cup cheese on the casserole and top with the biscuits. Or combine the cheese and crumbs and sprinkle on top. (Or the crushed potato chips if that's what you're in the mood for!)
6 Bake 25 to 35 minutes, until the filling bubbles, the cheese is melted, and the biscuits or crumbs are toasted.

Party Drinks . . . Not That You Need to Wait for a Party

BEER BLOODIES

A "splash" is ⅛ ounce (¾ teaspoon)—if you're measuring!

Makes 1 drink

4 ounces Bloody Mary mix, chilled (Fat and Juicy is my favorite brand!)
1½ ounces vodka
Ice cubes
Splash of olive juice
Splash of soda water, seltzer, or club soda
Splash of beer

GARNISHES (YOUR CHOICE)
Celery stalk
Lemon wedge
Lime wedge
Speared olive
Skewered boiled shrimp and cherry tomatoes

Combine the Bloody Mary mix, vodka, and ice in a cocktail shaker. Shake until condensation forms on the outside of the shaker. Strain into a tall glass with ice. Add the olive juice, soda water, and beer. Give a stir and serve with your choice of garnishes.

CHAMPAGNE COCKTAIL

Be sure the sparkling wine and soda are chilled well.

Makes 1 drink

Champagne or sparkling wine
1 ounce Italian blood orange or pomegranate soda

Garnish: Orange wedge, pomegranate seeds, candy cane

Fill a champagne flute two-thirds full with sparkling wine. Add the soda. Garnish with the fruit and a candy cane.

Variation: To make 24 cocktails, you'll need 4 bottles of Champagne or sparkling wine and one 25-ounce bottle Italian soda. Make each drink individually according to the directions above.

STRAWBERRY SPRITZER

Hull the strawberries after rinsing so the water does not rush into the berry and make it waterlogged and soggy.

Makes 1 drink

5 or 6 strawberries
1 teaspoon sugar
1½ ounces soda water, seltzer, or club soda
1 ounce vodka

3 ounces sparkling wine (prosecco, cava, or Champagne)
1 ounce strawberry soda or strawberry-flavored sparkling water

Ice cubes
Garnish: 1 whole strawberry

1 Rinse and drain the berries. Remove the leaves and hull and slice into a bowl. Sprinkle with the sugar to bring out the berry juices. Add the soda water and macerate about 10 minutes.

2 Mash with a fork or puree with an immersion blender. Add the vodka, wine, and strawberry soda. Mix well.

3 Pour, unstrained, over ice in a tall glass. Garnish with the whole strawberry.

SALTY DOG VODKA SODA

Makes 1 drink

1½ ounces vodka
1 ounce fresh grapefruit juice
Ice

Grapefruit slice, for rimming glass
1 teaspoon sugar
1 teaspoon kosher salt
⅛ teaspoon cayenne pepper

3 ounces soda water, seltzer, or club soda
Garnish: Lime half-slice

1 Combine the vodka, grapefruit juice, and ice in a cocktail shaker. Shake at least 25 times, until condensation forms on the shaker.

2 Rim the glass with the grapefruit slice. Combine the sugar, salt, and cayenne in a saucer. Dip the rim of the glass in the mixture. Put a few ice cubes in

the glass. Strain the drink into the glass, pour in the soda water, and garnish with the lime slice.

LIME BERRY COOLER

Makes 4 drinks

2 cups rinsed, hulled, and sliced
  strawberries
4 to 8 teaspoons Simple Syrup
  (pag 239)

4 teaspoons fresh lime juice
8 ounces tequila
Cracked or crushed ice

GARNISH
4 strawberries
4 lime wedges
4 fresh mint leaves

Puree the berries in a blender. Add the simple syrup, adjusting for the sweetness of the berries. Add the lime juice, tequila, and ice. Blend until frothy. Pour into 4 tall glasses. Garnish with fruit and a mint leaf.

MOREY MARGARITA

Makes 1 drink

4 slices cucumber
4 slices jalapeño chile
Ice cubes
1 ounce tequila

½ ounce orange liqueur
½ ounce fresh lime juice
½ ounce Simple Syrup (page
  239)

Lime wedge and kosher salt for
  rimming the glass
Garnish (optional): Fresh cilantro
  leaves

1 Put the cucumber and jalapeño slices in a cocktail shaker. Add a few ice cubes and shake until condensation forms on the shaker. Add the tequila, orange liqueur, lime juice, and simple syrup, fill with ice, and shake again.
2 Rim the glass with the lime wedge. Spread salt in a saucer, if using, and dip the rim of the glass in the salt. Fill the glass with ice and add a few cilantro leaves, if you like. Strain the drink into the glass or pour without straining, keeping the cucumber and jalapeño slices in the drink. Stir gently.

SIMPLE SYRUP

This syrup can keep in the refrigerator up to 1 month. It can be infused with mint, lime peel, lemon peel, or grapefruit peel.

Makes about 1 cup

1 cup water
1 cup sugar

Combine the water and sugar (and mint or citrus peel if infusing with a flavor) in a microwave-safe pitcher and microwave 2 minutes to dissolve the sugar. Let cool. Pour into a bottle, cap, and refrigerate.

PINK LEMONADE FROZEN MARGARITA

Make these without the tequila for the kiddos and add lemon slices dipped in pink sugar, umbrellas, and crazy straws to the garnish.

Makes about 1 quart, 4 to 6 drinks

1 (6-ounce) can frozen pink lemonade (not thawed)
2 cups crushed ice
6 ounces tequila
1½ ounces fresh lime juice

6 ounces plain soda water, seltzer, or club soda
6 ounces citrus-flavored soda water
Lime wedge, for rimming the glasses

2 tablespoons sugar
2 tablespoons kosher salt
Garnish: Fresh mint sprigs, fresh mint leaves, lime wedges

1 Combine the lemonade and ice in a blender and pulse to combine. Pour into a pitcher. Add the tequila and lime juice and mix well. Add the plain and flavored soda waters and mix gently.
2 Rim the glasses with a lime wedge. Combine the sugar and salt in a saucer. Dip the rims of the glasses in the mixture. Pour the margarita into the glasses and garnish with mint sprigs, mint leaves, and lime wedges.

AGUA FRESCA

Watermelon agua fresca can be used to fill popsicle molds or ice cube trays, or as a base for a watermelon margarita or watermelon mojito.

Makes 6 to 8 drinks

6 cups cubed seeded watermelon (about half a standard watermelon (not personal or seedless size), plus more for garnish
Grated zest and juice of 1 lemon
2 tablespoons to ¼ cup fresh mint leaves
Sugar or Simple Syrup (page 239), if needed
3 cups ice water
Optional: Kosher salt for rimming the glasses
Ice cubes
Garnish: Fresh mint sprigs

1 Puree the watermelon in a blender. Stir in the lemon zest, lemon juice, and mint leaves. Taste for sweetness and add sugar or simple syrup if needed. Strain (if you'd like) or pour into a tall pitcher. Add the ice water and refrigerate. Stir again before serving.

2 If you want to accent the flavor of the watermelon, dip the rims of the glasses in water, then in a saucer of salt.
3 Fill tall glasses with ice, pour in the agua fresca, and garnish with a fresh mint sprig and watermelon cubes.

FRENCH PRESS COFFEE

Makes 4 to 6 servings

1 quart water
4 to 5 tablespoons dark roast coffee beans
Pinch of kosher salt
Optional: Pinch of ground cinnamon

Bring the water to a boil. Grind the coffee beans and put in a French press pot. Add the salt. Add the cinnamon, if desired. Pour in the boiling water and brew 4 minutes. Gently push on the plunger until it reaches the bottom of the pot. Pour and enjoy.

SWEET TEA WITH MINT

Makes 2 quarts

2 quarts water
2 "family-size" tea bags
3 to 5 fresh mint sprigs
Sugar
Serving suggestion: Ice cubes, 2 lemons, thinly sliced

1 Bring the water to a boil.
2 Place the tea bags and mint in a 2-quart (or larger) heatproof pitcher. Pour in the water and let steep for 5 minutes.

3 Remove the tea bags. Stir in sugar to taste. Let cool to room temperature.
4 Serve over ice with lemon slices.

After more than five years in the making, I never thought I'd be here, writing acknowledgments for my very own cookbook!

There are so many people to thank:

To my mother, Callie, who taught me a love for all things food: She was the person who gave me the epiphany to share her fabulous biscuits with the world.

To my father, Donald, who always taught me that if I set my mind to it, I could do anything I wanted—and you know what? He was right. He has been and always will be the driving force behind any of my great accomplishments. I feel blessed to have been raised by such an amazing man.

To my grandmothers, Rebecca and Caroline, who instilled in me a deep love of Southern cooking and passed down an incredible food heritage.

To my three smart and beautiful children, Caroline, Cate, and Sarah, who have spent more hours with me in the kitchen than anyone— you make cooking fun (and messy!). I hope the memories of all our culinary afternoons will be ingrained in your minds forever.

To my husband, John, for his love, support, advice, and infinite patience at the dinner table while we waited to shoot every perfect photograph.

To my "biscuit babes" both paid and non-paid— you know who you are. ABK, KCH, and MBW,

you have entertained me on many a tasting trip, and you make it a joy to come to work every day! You have made it possible for me to focus on this book while you treated the biscuit business as your own. For that, I am forever grateful.

To my agent, Amy Hughes, who initially encouraged me to start writing about my food. I had no idea it would amount to this monumental project and new chapter in my life!

To Libba Osborne, the best publicist any girl could ask for . . . You've been there for the good and bad, and made this book shine!

To Leslie Meredith, who is an amazing, insightful editor; Donna Loffredo, who brilliantly connected all the dots; Jessica Chin, Dana Sloan, Julian Peploe, and Meghan Day Healey, who brought the book together on the page; and Jackie Jou and Cristina Suarez, who helped this book take flight.

To my writer, Bessie Gantt, who spent endless hours on the phone with me for months at a time. I told my tall tales and you spun those stories into the most perfect and authentic prose.

To my photographer, Angie Mosier, who made my simple Southern creations glamorous and drool worthy!

To Nathalie Dupree, a true mentor, for her overwhelming support and always inspiring and wise words.

To Deidre Schipani, my meticulous recipe tester. Thank you for your patience in taking a wealth of recipes that lived only in my head and beautifully translating them to paper. Cooking is easy for me—writing a recipe is the hard part!

Also to Laryn Adams at Chezelle clothing store in Charlotte, NC, for outfitting me so stylishly throughout the process of photographing this book.

Most of all, I want to thank all of the Callie's Biscuits fans—old and new. You made this book possible through your love of our handmade biscuits and spread the good word about our little company. You are the people who have made this a reality. Thanks y'all!

Index

255